RUNNER

---

*The inner quest of becoming a runner or athlete
or just about anything . . . at any age*

Jay Kimiecik
with
Doug Newburg

University Press of America,® Inc.
Lanham · Boulder · New York · Toronto · Plymouth, UK

Copyright © 2009 by
University Press of America,® Inc.
4501 Forbes Boulevard
Suite 200
Lanham, Maryland 20706
UPA Acquisitions Department (301) 459-3366

Estover Road
Plymouth PL6 7PY
United Kingdom

Library of Congress Control Number: 2009932202
ISBN: 978-0-7618-4795-3 (paperback : alk. paper)
eISBN: 978-0-7618-4796-0

Chapter 20 contains material reprinted with permission of Atria Books,
a Division of Simon & Schuster, Inc., from BOY'S LIFE by
Robert R. McCammon. © 1991 by the McCammon Corporation.

⊖™ The paper used in this publication meets the minimum
requirements of American National Standard for Information
Sciences—Permanence of Paper for Printed Library Materials,
ANSI Z39.48-1992

FOR
Carly and Colin
May they always be athletes

IN MEMORY OF
The 22 Bravest,
True Heroes

I think that what we're seeking is an experience of being alive, so that our life experiences on the purely physical plane will have resonance ... with our own innermost being and reality, so that we actually feel the rapture of being alive.

—Joseph Campbell

Tragedy arises when we are in the presence of a man who has missed accomplishing his joy.

—Arthur Miller

Whether I shall turn out to be the hero of my own life, or whether that station will be held by anybody else, these pages must show.

—Opening of *David Copperfield*
by Charles Dickens

CONTENTS

ILLUSTRATIONS

Figures

FOREWORD

"I am not an athlete."

These words began the first piece I ever wrote for *Runner's World* maga-zine. The story chronicled the experience of training for and running my first marathon at age 32, 4 days before my divorce to cyclist Lance Armstrong. Prior to that journey, I had supported, cared for, and cheered on a world-class athlete, but I did not consider the possibility of any athletic potential within the confines of my own body.

Since then I have completed 5 marathons, and will run my 2ⁿᵈ Boston Marathon in 2008, and I am now a Contributing Editor for *Runner's World*. I can relate to Jay in many ways; I attended Miami University and I too discov-ered my inner athlete later in life.

You know the feeling you get when you watch a sports highlights mon-tage, or view a spectacular performance in Olympic or Ironman television coverage? The choked up, holding your breath, skin has goose-bumps feeling? I have come to believe that we feel this way not because we are in awe of the power of another human being, but instead because we are reacting to a recognition of that same potential within our very selves. The potential means more to me than the performance. The authors refer to listening to the "little voice" of passion . . . and this is where cultivating courage and exploring endurance become very interesting to me. When our little voice begins to rise above the din of everyday existence we are reminded that none of us were ever destined to live an ordinary life.

We were designed to question and push our limits, in every sense, but pushing physical limits can become a metaphor for other areas in our lives to boldly follow suit. Our limits may not be as clearly ascertained as a recent P.R. in a half marathon, they may be as simple as overcoming the voice that tells us to stay on the sofa, that we were meant for the sidelines.

Jay's *Runner as Hero* encourages readers to "pay attention to how you want to feel." This gem of wisdom is pertinent to pursuing athletic vision, but the application goes far beyond that in reminding everyone at every level that we should *pay attention*. How do we want to feel in our jobs? In our relationships? In our very skin?

I hope you enjoy this book and are inspired to find and do the thing that reconnects you with your passion. Let your little voice be heard.

From one athlete to another,
Kristin Armstrong

INTRODUCTION

"Everyone has one great song to sing. It is their own story."
—Kris Kristofferson

This is a story about my quest to become a runner and athlete as I approached the cusp of middle age. It's a metaphorical attempt to explore what it means to live an engaged life and experience our potential no matter our age. In the story I play the role of participatory journalist/self-experimental, mad scientist—kind of a cross between George Plimpton and John Jerome, two of the late great masters of this sports writing genre. The main focus is on how you take an idea—in my case, become a middle-distance runner—and then live it out no matter your age. If you aren't a runner, don't be scared off by the fact that the story focuses mostly on my running experiences. The runner is just a metaphorical conduit for exploring the inner landscape of aging, training, and performing. I'd even venture to say that you don't need to become, or have to be, an athlete to gain something from the story but I think that's the trail many of us need to blaze to bring our minds and bodies back to life.

Runner as Hero is not a technical training book or a how-to-become-a-better runner or performer in six weeks. Plenty of experts are out there to help you with that. The problem with most of these expert-driven books, however, is that although on the mark technically the authors assume we are already as motivated as they are. I was more interested in taking a reflective step back and asking, "How does one build and sustain motivation and desire to perform in an activity of any kind?" Specifically, I asked, "How can I become an athlete as I get older? Why would I want to?"

Rather than being a technical treatise on running, *Runner as Hero* is more of a how to breathe life into an idea and live it over time. Having said that, I do think I've learned a thing or two from my own experiences, the experts, and the scientific literature about aging, running, and athletic performance that you may find interesting if not helpful. I knew very little about the art and science of aging or running when I started out so, hopefully, I've uncovered some things that might benefit your own race against time. Some of the human systems I focused on were physiological, biomechanical, musculoskeletal, neuromuscular, social, and psychological. I've attempted to weave the essence of what I found—as it pertains to aging, running, and becoming an athlete—throughout the book, but I hope that doesn't botch the story.

I am fearful that my story may not be dramatic enough. My quest didn't begin as a result of a major life crisis—no cancer to overcome, no dramatic weight loss, no bad marriage to escape from, no childhood scars. And I certainly didn't become a world champion masters athlete as a result of my quest. But isn't this the way it is for the vast majority of us. Aren't most of our lives lived in the gray area between intense joy and woeful melancholy? And yet each of our stories is unique and powerful no matter what the external results or outcomes might be. We each have a magic to be lived out no matter how much natural talent we may possess. And that is the real race against time—to find your bliss and live it no matter your age. With that in mind, I have sprinkled a few stories of other athletes—young and old—I met along the way to highlight ideas and concepts about feeling alive and getting good while growing old. Perhaps their stories will make up for my off-Broadway story and inspire you to explore your own ideas for feeling alive and getting good.

Doug Newburg is the co-author of *Runner as Hero*. I first met Doug when he was a performance educator with the surgery department at the University of Virginia's School of Medicine. He visited Miami University to speak at our sport and exercise psychology seminar and I was fascinated. The core principles of engaged living and optimal performance that emerge in this book are based on my interpretation of Doug's work with high-caliber performers from all walks of life. Doug knows more than anyone I know about what it takes to live an engaged, fulfilled life. Basically, he listens to your story and then helps you figure out how to feel alive, how to create and live your bliss. We have had hundreds of conversations over the years and those conversations served as the catalyst for me to dive into and explore my life as an athlete. Telling this story is my way of introducing you to what Doug knows and lives. My hope is that *Runner as Hero* will inspire you to undertake your own hero quest and live out that one great song in your heart.

WARMUP

"The first action or energy in making something a reality is an idea."
—Mike Stewart, former body boarding world champion

THE BIG IDEA

While I watched my son's soccer game, the idea hit me as hard as the Southwest Ohio rain that was pelting me. To distract me from the cold spring rain, I had been eavesdropping on two out of shape, boomer-age dads who were recounting their sports glory days in a blatant game of one-upmanship. Listening in I began to realize that at fortysomething my best athletic days were probably behind me as well. But did it have to be that way? The idea took shape in the form of a simple "What if?" What if I started training to become a runner, a real runner? Could I become an athlete again? Could I stay with it? Could I get good? How good? Would I need to become obsessed to get good? What would happen to my roles as husband, father, son, and professor? Was there room for the athlete in this spouse, two kids, dog and cat small-town life I was living? I had heard stories about middle-aged athletic obsession that led to divorces and other such messes. I wanted no part of that. I was happy with my life in general. But aren't most people? I didn't want to be happy; I wanted to be totally engaged in my life. I wanted to feel alive. My best guess was that becoming an athlete would wake me up.

While the two dads were reminiscing, I had a flashback of my own to a time when I was 11 or 12 participating in a Boy Scout camping jamboree in New York's Catskill Mountains. Part of the event was a troop-wide competition that included a variety of survival, sport, and water activities. One event was a 4-person running relay that wound through the woods on trails. I don't remember how far the course was but I was chosen for the third leg (my brother was the anchor). I received the baton from the second runner and took off. During the run, a feeling of power came over me that catapulted me through the woods. All I could hear were my breathing and my feet hitting the trail. I felt like I was floating even though the woods were a blur. Before I knew it, I heard "C'mon, Jay," from my brother. I handed him the baton and collapsed to the ground. I watched him take off and then lay there basking in my exhaustion. A few minutes later, I began the solitary walk to the finish line. I can't remember if we won or where we placed. I do remember feeling alive. I felt different. I felt like I had done something great. I had many more of those athlete-like feelings in my teens and twenties playing the typical American sports—soccer, basketball, baseball, to name a few. I wanted to feel that way again.

I wanted to get good at something physical; I wanted the feel of a performer; I wanted the look of an athlete, to be rid of the athletic malaise I was experiencing. But more than anything, I just wanted to bring me the athlete back to life. For most of us giving up on the athlete gets easier when we get jobs, get partners, get kids, get real. I was smack dab in the middle of all of it. You probably are too. So I began this adventure of rediscovering the athlete by becoming a runner.

I had been running off and on since my graduate school days and like many folks my age dabbled in a variety of sports—noontime basketball, golf, and tennis. But there was something about middle-distance running (mile, 1500, 5k) that kept invading my consciousness. I had decent speed and endurance, but wasn't a genetic freak with either. The idea turned into a simple goal: become a "competitive, age-group runner." I didn't have much racing experience, had never been a part of any kind of track and field team, and had never run an official race on a track. I'd have a lot to learn about running, about performing, about everything.

While a doctoral student at the University of Illinois, I achieved personal running bests the summer just after turning 30—a 5:06 in a July 4th mile road race and a sub 19:00 5K (3.1 miles) time. Shortly after my peak performance summer—which I credit to the enthusiasm of youth, not to the specificity of training principle—I developed the dreaded achilles tendonitis after some guy's shoe whacked me while playing basketball, moved to Oxford, Ohio to start my professor career at Miami University, welcomed two kids to the family in the mid 90s, got very sick with a viral infection of unknown origin, recovered, supported my wife as best I could as she began a job requiring travel, and got sucked up by work and life. (If this doesn't sound even remotely familiar, you can stop reading and go for a run or something.)

Suddenly it's the late 90s and as Forrest Gump once said, "Just like that, my running days was over." Oh, I was still running and racing a little but certainly not in a way that would qualify me as an athlete. I played basketball with colleagues at times and played with my two kids but I felt lost in my own body. My running days seemed over at least in the way I wanted them to feel. I felt more like the character Anne Tyler describes in the first line of her novel, *Back When We Were Grownups*, "Once upon a time there was a woman who discovered that she had turned into the wrong person." Well, I think this can happen to men too. It surely was happening to me. I was turning into the wrong person. I had once felt like an athlete. I didn't anymore.

I don't know why but the image of a hero setting out on a quest began to form in my consciousness. At first, I pushed this silly vision out of my head. I'm no hero, I thought. I'm just a fortysomething guy who wants to get the feel of being an athlete. By some divine intervention, I stumbled upon the late mythologist Joseph Campbell's Power of Myth while in our public library helping my daughter with a school project. Campbell helped me better understand the essence of a hero:

> *The usual hero adventure begins with someone from whom something has been taken, or who feels there's something lacking in the normal experiences available or permitted to the members of his society. The person then takes off on a series of adventures beyond the ordinary, either to recover what has been lost or to discover some life-giving elixir. It's usually a cycle, a going and returning.*

According to Campbell, everyone can—and should—be a hero because the hero is anyone who has the courage to take the journey to find what's missing, the "soul's high adventure," he calls it. Heroes go on the journey, not to save the world, but to save themselves. I knew the athlete part of my life was missing. I had to go out and find it.

THE ADVENTURE OF FEELING ALIVE BEGINS

It took me awhile to begin my quest following my spring awakening—a book to finish, teaching to do, yada, yada, yada. I started to quasi-train to be an athlete, meaning I just started running more. I ran in Cincinnati's Thanksgiving Day 10K race for the first time posting a 43:03. My comments in my journal were: "Ran well. Felt strong for first 10K in a long time." The result motivated me. *With some hard training maybe I really can do this*, I thought. In reality, I had no idea what I was doing.

Shortly after that race while running through knee pain yet again, I realized that I wasn't going to get very far in my quest on a bum knee. So only a short way from home, the adventure of the hero—the adventure of feeling alive—began.

LAP 1
ENGAGING IN PREPARATION

"That's when I decided I would always opt for expression over perfection."
—Yo Yo Ma

I toed the starting line of my 1,500-meter qualifying heat with nine other 45-59 year old feel seekers at the USA Masters Outdoor Track and Field Championships. My head was filled with nagging thoughts and questions: *Am I a real runner? Who are these guys? They look damn serious and damn good. Where are you, Pre?*

The gun went off. I immediately fell near the back of the pack as I knew I would. *Relax. No big deal.* I cruised the first lap in 76, just a second over my goal pace. I was in last place but that didn't bother me. *This seems pretty easy. I'm used to racing against myself anyway . . .*

1
THE LITTLE VOICE OF FEEL

"Well, Jay, you have patello-femoral dysfunction," the doc said after viewing my X-rays and palpating my knee as if he was kneading raw meat. Patello-femoral dysfunction is the medical term used to cover just about anything wrong with the knee that doesn't require surgery. Why is medical terminology always so negative? Dysfunction? That makes me feel real good about myself.

"So what should I do about it?" I asked.

"Well, you should start in with physical therapy to strengthen the inner leg and to increase your flexibility. And if I were you I would cut back on the running for awhile."

"Do I have to stop running?" was my knee-jerk response.

"Well, you don't *have* to, but this has been a chronic condition that won't get better unless you nip it in the bud now. Why did you wait two years to see someone for it?"

Because I'm dysfunctional?

"Uh, I don't know."

I always seem to be the last one to know or do anything. When you're not sure about who you are or what you want, procrastination takes center stage.

My injury was right in line with the research on older athletes. A study out of the University of Rochester found that athletes over forty experience injuries associated with internal derangement of the knee, patellofemoral pain syndrome, and inflammation (e.g., tendonitis) much more frequently than younger athletes. So is it a syndrome or a dysfunction, not that it matters.

About a week later, I walked my syndrome self into physical therapy (novelist Stephen King, who had to rehabilitate from a life-threatening accident, accurately labeled it Pain and Torture) for the first time ever. Most of the patients seemed a bit on the antiquish side. As I waited I scanned some of the photos of athletes on the walls. The one that stood out was of Wally

Szcerbiak, a Miami University graduate who went on to play in the National Basketball Association.

Man, I just want to get back in the game, said my little voice of bliss. *I want to be up front in the race. I want to be like these athletes. I want to be up on the wall.*

My bigger voice retorted: AH, FORGET ABOUT IT. NO ONE GIVES A HOOT ABOUT YOU AND YOUR QUEST TO BE AN ATHLETE AGAIN. YOU HAD YOUR CHANCE. JUST GO BACK TO THE OFFICE AND GET SOME REAL WORK DONE. OR BETTER YET, JOIN A COMMITTEE AND PRETEND THAT YOU'RE WORKING!

Shut up, my little voice said to my bigger voice.

I could see that I was going to have to work on making my little voice a lot bigger if I was to carry out this quest. How does one bring passion—the little voice—alive and then sustain it? The self-help gurus talk about the importance of passion but no one can really help you get it but yourself.

For me, it seemed to come down to one key principle: to become an athlete, to become a performer, I needed to focus on *feel*. I was going on the notion that the little voice of the athlete is made bigger by experiencing a feel you like to have in the moment of action, whether it be training, performing, or competing. If you're not experiencing the feel you like to have when you train, for example, you aren't going to do it no matter how great the training program might be. You won't sustain the motivation. And if you don't experience that feel when competing, you're probably not going to perform very well. Of course, the people who develop all of these great training programs seem to side step or ignore this most important piece of performance information. People buy the books thinking they can side step it as well and find out shortly after the book is not all that helpful in the long haul. I wanted a feel of speed, of freedom, of push. This is when I felt most alive. No training program, no book can provide that. I had to create this feel for myself. It's the only way to sustain anything.

I knew from my work and friendship with Doug that outstanding performers focus much more on how they want to feel in the moment of action than on potential outcomes or goals. In my head I understood the principle, but I needed to experience it. When I first started this quest, Doug just said, "pay attention."

"Pay attention to what?" I asked.

"Pay attention to how you want to feel," he replied.

"But I'm not quite sure what that is."

"Exactly. That's why you need to pay attention."

"Oh."

Mihalyi Csikszentmihalyi, one of the early leaders in studying the inner landscape of optimal experiences, writes that people's talents develop when their involvement in an activity is both satisfying at the moment *and* promising of long-term rewards. You must have a feel of engagement in the moment of action to continue in any activity and to perform your best. If you don't, your idea of becoming an athlete—at any age—will remain in your head unlived. Eventually you'll forget about it or it will just die off, and you'll live vicariously through the athletic lives of your kids and grandkids. But watching athletes and living the feel of the athlete for yourself are not the same thing.

2
WHY ATHLETE

Athlete is a word bantered about quite a bit these days by corporate trainers, sports announcers, and writers. One trend is this idea of the corporate athlete, where executives should train in the same systematic way as professional athletes, as if training systematically makes one an athlete. Applying a few athlete-type principles—discipline, commitment, blah, blah, blah—in your daily life does not make you a athlete. Plus, I'm not convinced that you can just take these "athlete lessons" and apply them in your daily life without actually experiencing them on the playing field. I'm sure many will disagree (especially some self help writers and corporate trainers). But playing a sport periodically with friends does not make one an athlete; training like an athlete does not make you an athlete. It sounds nice and all—and probably sells books—but it doesn't resonate. Something is missing.

Out of curiosity, I started hunting down definitions of *athlete*. I realized post haste that this was a mistake. Writing in the scientific journal *Circulation*, the American Heart Association Science Advisory states that a competitive masters athlete is generally anyone from 35 to 100 years old who participates in an organized team or individual sport that requires regular competition against others, places a high premium on excellence and achievement, and requires systematic training. That's it? No way. What about love, passion, enjoyment, transformation? Surely there must be more to being an athlete than competing, performing, and training. Competing alone does not make one an athlete; training in and of itself does not make one an athlete; placing a premium on excellence and achievement does not make one an athlete. This definition says nothing about the individual experience. It says nothing about what is going on in your inner world when you are competing, performing, and training. It says nothing about transformation of consciousness, about building the way of the athlete into one's life until it is who you are.

To be an athlete, you have to build it into your life. It has to be sustainable

over time. That is what I wanted to do. I wanted the feel of an athlete and I
wanted it on a regular basis. I didn't just want to compete, to train, to perform. I went searching for thinkers and writers who might be able to help me
get a better handle on what I was after in becoming an athlete.

The late John Jerome, who chronicled his experiences in becoming a masters athlete in *Staying With It*, writes:

> *There comes a time, however, when you have to take a larger bite. You have to
> start trying to apply the pressure every step, every stroke. You can't, of course;
> you fail, frequently at first, less often as you get more familiar with what is
> required to stay with the effort. But you have to begin to try. It is not a physical
> transition, it is entirely in your mind. I believe that the moment you make that
> transition is the moment you become an athlete.*

Jerome's view seems closer to the idea of the athlete I had been envision-
ing. Many years ago George Leonard wrote *The Ultimate Athlete*, which he
considered to be mythical and an ideal. But a part of the ultimate athlete
experience was when one "surpasses limitations and crosses boundaries in
the process of personal and social transformation." Now you can train and
compete all you want and not become transformed. Leonard writes, "But the
body of the Ultimate Athlete—fat or thin, short or tall—summons us beyond
these things toward the rebirth of the self, and, in time, the unfolding of a
new world." You become an athlete when you are transformed into a new
being as a result of the emotional and mental process of training, competing,
and performing. That is what I was after. And my guess is that when this
transformation or rebirth of the self occurred, I would be more likely to tap
into my God-given potential. Sport lays the groundwork for this transformation to occur but there is certainly no guarantee you'll experience it just by
participating. That's why the typical definition of athlete—one who takes part
in competitive sports—doesn't tell us much.

We have to dig deeper. According to THE source—the *Oxford English
Dictionary*—sport is:
- **Diversion from serious duties; relaxation, recreation; entertainment,
  amusement.**
- **Anything which affords diversion and entertainment; a pastime, game, sport.**
  Notice that originally sport was defined more by its mental or emo-
  tional characteristics than by the physicality of the activities. Exercise,
  on the other hand, is:
- **Practice for the sake of training or improvement, either bodily, mental,
  or spiritual.**

Sport is a diversion, something we mentally experience. By definition, it is
a mental experience. Exercise, on the other hand, has a different purpose—to
work, to train, to prepare for a result or outcome. Exercise can be done as a

way of improving mental or physical health, even spirituality, but the mental aspects are not part of the definition.

People who exercise on a regular basis cannot understand why many people just won't get off the couch and exercise. But for most people, including me, what is missing from exercise *is* sport. Psychologically, exercise and sport are completely different. By becoming an athlete, you put sport into exercise. And how do you do that? You have to know how you want to feel. You have to approach it voluntarily. You have to give yourself up to it. This helps to keep your training and practice from turning into exercise.

And then there's the competition. According to the *Oxford English Dictionary*, to compete is to strive with another. Even more fascinating is the idea that the word competence is associated with compete. In other words, competition is designed to *increase the competency of the competitors*, not merely arrive at an outcome in which someone is a winner and someone is a loser.

Sport is by definition something mental, something diversionary, less serious, something maybe even voluntarily undertaken. It is why we do it, not what we do. Exercise is the act of preparing, training, doing the work, practicing with a specific purpose or outcome. This is working with a goal in mind in a loose translation. But if you don't bring yourself into exercise or don't know how you want to feel or express yourself, you probably won't sustain it. That's where the athlete, sport, and competition come into the picture. Face it: being an athlete, participating in sport, getting good are all harder than exercising but a lot more fun. Why? *Because you are more likely to express yourself in the activity.* So the key is to find what that is for you, create it, and nurture it. Becoming an athlete via sport and competition are much more likely to do that than exercise and fitness. Competing helps you turn exercise into sport and makes it a lot more interesting, which means you'll probably do it more, even though it's harder than exercise. Eleanor Metheny writes about the rules and the power of sport in her essay *The Symbolic Power of Sport:*

> *These rules are paradoxical. They restrict in order to free. They impose restrictions on human behavior and they limit human action, but within those restrictions they offer every man an opportunity to know the feeling of being wholly free to go all out- free to do his utmost- free to use himself fully in the performance of one self chosen human action.*

As we get older there is a tendency to lose that feeling of freedom, to go all out, to go after something with everything you've got. Aging experts John Rowe and Robert Kahn pointed out in their popular book *Successful Aging* that as many people move into middle age they begin to lose feelings of competence and autonomy. And psychologists Ed Deci and Richard Ryan write that these basic human feelings are essential for optimal health and well-being. I knew I was losing these. I needed to venture out into the world to rediscover them and, in my case, I had a hunch that the intersection of athlete, sport, and competition was where I would experience them again. I went after the athlete.

3
THE WEAKEST LINK

I was finding early in my quest that living the athlete's way required a lot of preparation if I was going to be able to tap into my running potential. I tried to stick with my key principle: engage in whatever I was doing to get the feel I wanted. That wasn't too easy at first since I was spending a lot of my time in activities other than running.

I found one quote by a group of medical experts writing in *Sports Medicine* particularly thought-provoking: "Since a chain breaks at the weakest link, the masters athlete must do his or her best to minimize the stress on the known weak links." I was learning from physical therapists, podiatrists, and my own experiences that my weakest link to becoming a real runner was my legs (not good), partly because of past trauma but also due to a funky leg structure. I was placed in a patello-femoral protection program—appropriate as no one really knew who I was or what I was doing including myself—because of my weak inner thigh muscles and tighter-than-a-Titleist musculature. This combination was causing my left knee's patella to track out of its groove. To add to my woe, my legs rotated inward when I ran, and since my inner thigh muscles weren't strong enough to hold the patella in place, it rotated outward (every action has an equal and opposite reaction) pulling on tendons and soft tissue as it went. As some runners know, this experience causes one to say "ouch!" with every foot strike.

Here is one podiatrist's evaluation of my weak link:

John Jay Kimiecik is a college professor suffering from peri patellar tendonitis on the left knee when he runs.

Videotaped biomechanical evaluation reveals a predisposition to this condition based on the findings that his left leg is long and both his feet spend too much time in the shock absorbing phase. This causes the lower shin to internally rotate excessively as the center of gravity passes over the leg while the foot is locked on the ground. This causes excessive micro repetitive over use to the knee cap and it is now inflamed.

A pair of L3010 full length prescription casted suborthalene orthotics with an intrinsic fore foot varus post and a heel lift on the short right side will cause his phases of heel contact, shock absorption, adaptation, stance, and propulsion to take place at the correct time interval. By doing this, the excessive internal tibia rotation will be decreased and slowed down and this greatly reduces the stress at the knee.

The weak link idea struck me as a metaphor for living and performing our best. How many times do we avoid our weak points because we are afraid of what we might find out? But to get better at anything, we must make our weak link stronger. I kept going with the patella protection program—stretching and strengthening the leg muscles—because I didn't know what else to do.

4
PAYING ATTENTION IN PREPARATION

A couple of times each day I performed basic stretches for the quads, hamstrings, calves, and hip flexors. The idea, as I vaguely understood it, was to lengthen the muscles to take some of the pressure off of the kneecap when I ran. The strengthening exercises were just as basic—some straight leg raises and squeezing a towel with my thighs. At first, my attitude was, "What good will these activities do? Could this be any more boring?" But after awhile, the stretching began to feel good. I looked forward to the peacefulness of each stretch and that little bit of pull—just enough to make you pay attention. The stretching was my form of meditation. It was my quiet time—early in the morning before the chaos of the day and late at night when it had ended. The strengthening exercises were more challenging than I thought they would be. Squeezing a towel in between your thighs and holding it for 2-3 seconds thirty to fifty times takes some concentration. And raising your leg and holding it up for a few seconds while contracting the thigh muscle is not something you can do while whistling. I got interested in the challenge and was motivated by the thought that the increased quad strength would get my patella to track in its groove. I thought of it as getting my groove back.

Shortly after I began physical therapy, I figured I should get a baseline measure of my overall strength as a quasi-scientific means of gauging my development over time. I convinced Miami University's Strength and Conditioning Coach to take me through a battery of strength tests. I met Coach at the student-athlete strength and conditioning facility. Coach is a former football player and larger than life. I found out later he was an outstanding athlete at Miami and had been inducted into our Hall of Fame. After explaining to Coach what I was trying to do, he came up with 8 tests that would give me a general measure of overall body strength and power: vertical jump, standing long jump, leg press, bench press, medicine ball chest pass, push ups, chinups, and situps. I didn't question the selection as I was just happy that someone was putting up with my self-experimentation.

My performance was abysmal. I ended the tests with only being able to do 6 pushups, 8 situps in 60 seconds, and 1 chinup. I thanked Coach, apologized for performing so poorly, and told him that I'd be back in a few months for a retest. I hobbled out into the cold feeling about as strong as a broken jock strap.

On the brighter side, I was impressing my physical therapist with my progression. One day after another quality physical therapy performance, he said, "Well, Jay, it's time to get you in the water."

"Say what?"

5

WATER WORLD

Water and I have a long history of not getting along. As a child, I flunked a swim test at the local pool and could not advance with my friends to the next level. In college, I almost flunked a required swim class, which was taught by the swim coach, because I couldn't perform some kind of frog kick. He actually made me come to the pool on a Saturday morning to demonstrate this kick for him. Flunk him! I once had to swim two lengths of a pool so I could join the Purdue University Sailing Club (for reasons that are too embarrassing to divulge but they did involve the woman who is now my wife). I finished dead last by a wide margin and then almost drowned when I had to perform a treading-water test (true story).

Despite these fears, I showed up at Miami University's Recreational Sports Center at the scheduled time for my aqua therapy, which is getting more popular in rehab circles. There's a good reason for this: water is denser than air and offers greater resistance to movement—drag—while at the same time unloading the joints—low impact. You can get stronger more quickly in an environment that's easy on your body. You can wear flotation belts to completely unload the joints—no impact. To add to the beauty, water work reduces pain and swelling and increases circulation and freedom of movement. Water exercise is so popular now that it has gone way beyond rehab only. A study in *Medicine and Science in Sports and Exercise* found that a 12-week water program for 60- to 75-year old women that included walking and dancing in chest-deep water increased muscular strength, oxygen uptake, flexibility, agility, and fat loss. No injuries were reported. Professional athletes are also using water as part of rehab because it gets them back in the lineup faster. According to the experts, an athlete who is immersed at neck level in water is only 10% of normal body weight. Three hundred pounds is reduced to 30 pounds. Water exercise seems to be ideal for these three categories: older adults, injured adults, injured athletes, and I was in all three.

When I saw that the leisure pool was four feet at the deepest end, I felt better and my fear of drowning diminished. My aqua therapist, Lara, started me off with the basics: walking forwards and backwards, walking side to side, and some stretching. Then I started in on the real leg work: a series of toe raises and side and back leg raises while standing on a step. Then it got a little harder. I had to balance on a buoy and mimic a squat motion by pushing the buoy down into the water with my legs and then releasing up. The capper was a series of squats on three steps that bridged the baby pool and the leisure pool. On each step, I had to balance on one leg and then squat to drop the other leg below the step and then come back up. I was to do 15 reps on each of the three steps for each leg. The challenge was to not lose my balance during the 15 reps. Near the end of the session, Lara gave me a floatation belt and told me to do some running in the deepest part of the leisure pool. "Have some fun," she said. So I started running. I felt the rapture of being alive. I wanted to run forever.

In addition to my weekly aqua therapy sessions, about once a week I would strap on a flotation belt and jump in the Rec Center's main pool, which is Olympic size and quite jazzy. Sometimes Luann, the fitness center director and former marine, would instruct me on technique, other times I'd be on my own. I took in lots of water in my first session as I learned how to perform butt-kickers, x-country and jumping jacks pop ups, high knee marches, toe-touches, and others I can't recall. I felt as goofy as Sponge Bob. Afterwards I overheard an older woman who had been participating in a water aerobics class next to my lane ask Luann, "Are you teaching that nice young man how to swim?"

On my final day of aqua therapy I cranked on all of my strengthening activities and did the entire series of step squats without needing to hold on to the rail for balance. I was in the physical therapy zone. Water and I were getting along. Near the end of the session, I rested in my glory and watched a group of three older guys who had been coming together to therapy the past few weeks. They always had fun interacting with each other. Today they were messing around shooting baskets at the pool's hoop until Lara had to yell at them in a motherly way to stop goofing around and get back to work. My bygone basketball days were urging me to join them as I heard the echoes of my old high school gym. Talk about feeling alive! The old gym was so small that the half-court and foul-line circles were no more than a foot apart. A player with a good long range jump shot would be barely over half court before firing away. What really made the court shrink were the dusty gray mats that hung from the brick wall just beyond each baseline. These mats served as the baseline and were there to protect players from crashing into solid brick. Bordering one side of the court was the stage with stairs jutting out on to the court on both sides. Sitting in the first row of the stairs, you could reach out and touch a player shooting a baseline jumper. A concrete balcony hovered over the court on the other side. If you were in the first row balcony, you felt as if you were playing in the game. Because of the brick walls—and proximity of the crowd—cheers and boos were greatly amplified. I can still hear, "Munch, munch, munch, the ref brought his lunch, eat it ref, eat it!" Everyone was part of the action and emotions ran high because of it. In February of my senior year, we moved the action to the new gym in the new elementary school. The games just didn't feel the same.

I never did join the three older hoopsters. As I thanked Lara and left the water world behind, I felt alone, inadequate, and not quite sure where this quest was taking me next. I wanted to be a runner but I didn't feel like one. I wanted to feel like I did in the old gym. Could I relive the glory days or should I just grow up and act my age?

6
GETTING TO THE CORE OF THE MATTER

In the heart of winter, I had started running outside again a couple of days a week. I felt slow. My legs had gotten used to the water and I was unprepared for the concrete pounding. The first time out, my legs were actually sore and stiff the next day. I had been doing some reading about this thing called core or whole body fitness and how it can help athletes. I needed to start some weight training anyway, so I set up a meeting with Luann. She suggested that I begin with some basic core strength exercises involving the stability ball and balance board. I had always been a natural with hand-eye coordination, agility, and balance. But I had never really thought about my body as a whole unit. Luann started me off with some basic core activities: squats, supine pull ups, dumbbell chest press, and pushups. The difference was that I would do these activities while standing on a balance board or using a stability ball. The squats, for example, had me standing on a balance board with a stability ball resting between my back and the wall. I had to squat to about a 90 degree angle and hold for 10 seconds before coming back up. The pain and torture was alive and well. The balance board is used to make the squats more difficult, thereby increasing the pain and torture. As my legs were quivering, Luann told me that I would eventually add dumbbells into the squat. I just nodded. The ball was also being used to exponentially increase the pain and torture quotient. Regular pushups are far more difficult when trying to balance your legs on a ball while going up and down with the upper body.

I'm making it sound hard, and it was, but I took to core training like a beat up runner to a massage. In all of these exercises, my body was being forced into a high degree of coordination while working on both muscle strength and endurance. My body awareness, otherwise known as proprioception, was being raised from the dead. With some injuries, the trauma to the tissues can lead to proprioceptive deficits. This can delay recovery if not addressed and put an athlete at greater risk of reinjury when he or she returns to action. If we begin to lose that neuromuscular connection as we get older, whatever we can do to hold on to it or bring it back to life is essential for optimal performances and injury prevention and recovery. If you have decrements in your neuromuscular pathways, your rehabilitation from most injuries will be slow. The core training was helping me get a sense of my body again; it was helping me gain what scientists call joint sense awareness. The basic idea is that we need a rigid center of support to help the peripheral muscles move most effectively. A person who works to optimize abdominal, hip, and back strength—the core—should have better performance in the arms and legs in a variety of athletic activities. In addition, core fitness works to keep the spine in a neutral position, which decreases lower back pain problems. It keeps your torso erect, which is important in many athletic activities. For example, you want a "tall spine" when running as that position optimizes oxygen uptake. Angela Smith, a past president of the American College of Sports Medicine, was quoted in a *Newsweek* article: "If you don't have power in your spine and your trunk, you can't throw hard, you can't run fast." The point: work the whole body if you want to be at your athletic best and prevent injury.

In early winter, my training was interrupted by a bad case of hives. I actually had to go to the emergency room and get pumped full of epinephrine. As is usually the case, the cause was never determined. As I lay there in a drug-induced stupor, I floated in and out of dreams. I found myself running on a track with Steve Prefontaine, the great American runner who ran for the University of Oregon in Eugene and dominated middle distance events until a tragic car crash ended his life in 1975 at age 24. We were side by side when Pre spoke[1]:

"So you want to be a runner?" he asked
"Well, not so much a runner as an athlete."
"They're the same thing."
"What do you mean?" I asked
But before I could get an answer, Pre waved and ran out of my subconscious.

What was that about, I wondered?

It took a few days to recover from the hives, but when I did I pounded into my training with gusto. In the back of my mind I was wondering if all of this core training would really make me a faster runner. What I concluded eventually is not that core training made me a faster runner per se but it allowed me to run without breaking down so that I could practice to get faster. Core training was my performance life preserver.

By late winter I was full bore into my training. A typical week included core training, running, cross-training in the water, and a couple of rest days. I was feeling stronger. I was coming alive. In my follow-up strength test, I improved dramatically on all 8 fitness tests and maxed out at 13 pushups, 14 situps, and 4 chinups. Coach kept saying, "very impressive, very impressive."

My jock strap was fixed.

So if you don't want to become an athlete you can stop here. If you do some basic core training, aerobic exercise, and some pool work, you can get fit and studly looking. And your knees will be forever grateful. Of course, this has been the prescriptive meal fed to us for years by public health and exercise experts without much success. I think the athlete component is what's missing for most people—testing, pushing, competing, paining, a feel of engagement, of being alive. That's why athletes keep coming back day after day, for all of it—the good, the bad, the ugly—because they love all of it. I forged ahead to experience the athlete.

Notes

1. Quotes attributed to Steve Prefontaine at http://www.stevepre.com were used in some of the dialogue I had with Pre's ghost. Tom Jordan's biography *Pre* also was helpful in directing my conversations with Pre's ghost.

7

I AM LADY HEAR ME ROAR

One observation that kept staring me square in the face was that I always worked harder and better in the water when Lara was working one-on-one with me. And this was definitely the case when Luann helped me in the pool or in the weight room. I performed and felt better in the presence of another human being. Part of it was getting quality feedback on my technique. Once we get into a routine with weights, for example, the danger is just that—routine. Over time, the correct movement deteriorates or we get a little lazy when on our own. I suggest that you fess up to this universal feedback principle of performance. If you don't, your improvement will be delayed or performance will plateau or you will get hurt.

Luann was watching me do my calf raises on the calf machine. I had been doing this exercise for a few months on my own most of the time. I thought I was doing them right. After a few calf raises, Luann said, "Stop, get off the machine. Stand and face me." I obeyed like a puppy that had just crapped in the house. Making sure I was paying attention, Luann gave her orders: "Now lift up as high as you can on your toes." I went up as high as I could a couple of times. "Yes, yes, that's it!" Luann said with her typical enthusiasm. "Now that's as high as you need to go when you're doing them on the machine. You're not going high enough and it's at the highest point when you are getting the most out of the movement. That's especially important for you with your funky legs."

I got back on the machine and consciously focused on pushing my toes all the way through to get as high as I could. After a few reps I could feel the difference. Wow! Hot fire down below! My technique had been all wrong. I had been unwittingly going through the motions. I had been taking the path of least resistance. All of this had occurred because I wasn't paying attention. I didn't know or had forgotten what the correct calf raise should feel like. I needed the feedback to get back on track.

So getting good feedback from an expert—at least every now and then—is an important part of the social dynamics of quality performance. This notion of performing better when being guided by an expert made me mad at first because I felt as a budding athlete I should be able to give the same quality effort when working out by myself as when I was with someone. But I couldn't. Eventually I just accepted it as fact and starting sniffing around the literature pertaining to relationships, aging, and performance. What I found was enlightening and frightening at the same time. Having quality relationships is one of the most significant factors for what gerontologists call successful aging (enlightening), and I do not have many of what I would call quality relationships at the moment (frightening) outside of my wife and kids. I don't know about you, but I have lots of colleagues and few real friends. Colleagues are people you have to work with, friends are people who help you enjoy life. My lack of friends may not be optimal for my health or my performance. A study in the *Journal of Gerontology* showed that men and women, aged 70-79, who had a high level of emotional support from their social network performed better on a series of physical tests than those with low support. Better support, better performance no matter your age. And the results of studies on older adults demonstrate that strong relationships can biologically age individuals at a slower rate. One study found that across different age groups, those people with high levels of social support had lower blood pressure than those with low levels of support.

I wanted to perform and train my best, and my experiences with my trainers as well as the science were telling me one thing: I'd better find a team of some kind. But where does a fortysomething, wannabe runner/professor living in small town USA find a team with which to run and train? I didn't have much leisure time due to work and family responsibility (my wife's travel with her job makes me the primary caregiver to our two children most days of the week). I considered talking to the men's track and field coach at Miami, but I quickly thought better of it. I wasn't a complete idiot—there was no way I could keep up with Division I male college-level runners. I was already an injury waiting to happen without begin dumb about it. But . . . what about the women? Not to be sexist, but I knew my times would be more in line with theirs. I emailed the women's coach at Miami and he welcomed me on board.

On my first day at the track in early spring, Coach Ceronie half-jokingly introduced me as an "old fart" to the team and then I began my first-ever interval work experience as a "member" of a team. I found out immediately that female track athletes are very supportive of each other. When circling the track with a pack of middle-distance runners, all I kept hearing from the other runners was "good job, ladies," "way to go, ladies." This was my introduction to being part of team. I was now a lady.

My first track interval experience in quite a few years was a 2 x 400, 1 x

800, 2 x 400. The following week, I did a 1x1000, 1x800, 1x600, 1x400. I didn't really know exactly why I was doing interval work. But my instincts were right in that being part of a quasi-team was uplifting. Running with the pack gave me a feeling of power and invincibility even though I was always in the back of the pack. Of course, there are worse things in life than running behind athletic, young women (a female friend of mine believes to this day that this was the sole source of my motivation, which I deny as strongly as former President Clinton denied you know what). Even though I was relatively slow on the track, the feeling of engagement was immediate. I loved everything about the oval—the forgiving surface, the conciseness of time, the speed, the push, the burn, the recovery in between each interval. Coach Ceronie would talk to the team about threshold, tempo, 85% and 90% of maximum heart rate, etc. Much of this went in one ear and out the other. I just tried to run fast and keep up with whomever on the team was last. One day each week, I showed up, shut up, and performed to the best of my ability. It was exhilarating.

Throughout the spring, I enjoyed being in my preparation phase of becoming an athlete—rehab, core training, water work, running, and the interval work. I was finding a feeling of engagement in the pain of preparation. But to be a real performer, you can't stay in the preparation phase. You can't continually prepare for something without experiencing that something. You can't live in your head all of your life like a scientist. You have to get out there and test yourself against yourself and others. That's what athletes do. That's where transformation takes place. So I began to race.

LAP 2
EMBRACING PAIN AND DISCOMFORT

"If you have a body, you are an athlete."
         —Bill Bowerman
           Legendary University of Oregon track coach
           and Nike co-founder

. . . Keep the pace. Stay strong. Stay smooth. This is starting to hurt. The pain means nothing. It's a sign you're pushing. That's what you want. I was still in last place but not far behind the guy just in front of me. *Keep him close. Man, my throat is dry.* Two laps down and the electronic timer showed 2:32. *Okay, another 76. Good pace. Stay tall. Here we go. The pain is coming . . .*

8

THE SUMMER OF PAIN

"C'mon, Jay, push it. Your pace is slowing up. This is where you are slowing down in races too. *You've got to push through the discomfort.*" From his
bike patrol perch, Coach Ceronie was doing his best to motivate me. I was at
about mile 3 of a 4.75 mile time trial on the roads with Miami's women cross
country runners, most of whom had surged ahead of me. I had just run up
what seemed like Mt. Rushmore. I was waxed. It was late summer and it was
hot, even at 8:00 a.m.

"I'm slowing up because there is nothing there," I gasped. "I ran five miles
yesterday. I think my legs are just wiped."

"No excuses," Coach fired back. "You wouldn't be saying that if you were
20 years old would you?"

"I can't even remember when I was 20 years old."

"You've got a downhill coming up. Really push down the hill. Catch
somebody." And then he sped away to meet his runners at the finish.

Of course, I didn't catch anyone. Near the end of the run, I ran by the
fields where my son was playing a soccer game. I looked for him, desperate for
some family connection to ease the pain. I couldn't find him and tears welled
up. As I arrived at the finish, Coach said: "33:15. Pretty good, but you can do
better. You're in better shape than what your time shows. You've got to push
through the discomfort in the middle of these runs." I nodded but had no
foggy idea how to do that.

The entire summer I had trained and raced without much apparent outward progress. When I started running road races after my physical therapy
and water rehab, my times did not match my expectations—in between 20:30
and 21:00 (about a 6:40 per mile pace) for the 5Ks. In early summer, my first
mile race in 14 years was a blistering 5:49 on the road (and that was with a
slight downhill the last quarter mile). I'm sure my expectations were too high
and I had been warned by the writings of other masters athletes that this is a

trap to avoid—expecting too much too soon.

On a humid summer evening I ran another mile road race in Cincinnati. I emailed a couple of my Cincinnati friends letting them know of my race plans on the possibility that they might show up as raving fans. One friend emailed back: "Man, you must be really motivated to drive an hour to run in a race that lasts about six minutes." I had to laugh at his insight. I was finding that being an athlete is not rational. I bribed my family with dinner out afterwards if they came with me. We drove an hour in heavy rain, thunder, and lightning. My wife, Kim, asked, "Are you sure you want to do this?" Meaning, "even though I love you I think you are nuts." I had to agree with her to a certain extent. I was still searching for the deeper, inner reasons for this quest. And my fear was that until I found them, I would be empty in races when I needed to dig deep. I was afraid there would be nothing there.

My time for the mile that evening was 5:17. I tried to ignore the fact that the race had a steep downhill component to it. But I was getting faster in the mile races and liking it. I saw a glimmer of hope. At dinner afterwards with my family and the two friends who actually showed up to cheer me on, I devoured my meal and felt like a caveman after the kill. Two more 5ks in August had me stuck on 20:56. All I can remember of these races is blistering heat, the infamous rolling hills, and succumbing yet again to the pain and discomfort. In these races I would begin to run out of gas midway through. I felt slow. I felt old. I did not feel like a performer. Was it my training? Was it my age? Was I expecting too much, too soon? Was my brain drying up like a raisin in the sun?

What does actually happen to the brain and motivation as we get older? Cognitive vitality does decline. Our brains atrophy and we lose synapses and neurons and a lot of other things only a neuroscientist can understand. But the cognitive decline does not have to be as severe as we might think. Neuronal loss and brain cell death is no longer thought to be an inevitable characteristic of aging. According to a group of neuroscientists writing in the *Mayo Clinic Proceedings*, the ones who keep the cognitive vitality have what is called *functional reserve* in their brains. Many ways are being uncovered to enhance cognitive vitality for older adults, but one of the best seems to be good, old-fashioned exercise. For example, it appears that running enhances neurogenesis in both mice and humans and that these new brain cells increase the plasticity of the brain. What we get is improved learning and better cognitive performance.

So it didn't seem likely that an atrophying brain was the cause of my less-than-stellar performances. In fact, just the opposite: with all of the physical activity I was doing, my brain was on overdrive most of the time. I kept coming back to Coach Ceronie's words, "you have to push through the discomfort." I knew he was right but how? I had been an athlete once upon a time but mostly in team sports. I knew how to suck it up in the last quarter of a basketball or soccer game. I knew how to push myself and my teammates when the going got tough. But I had no idea how to push through discomfort to run faster. I started digging around again. I stumbled upon a website article on the *Psychology of Competition* posted by Bob Schul, the 1964 Olympic gold medalist (and a Miami University alum) in the 5000 meters. He writes,

> *It is not enough to have the body in great cardiovascular condition. A top athlete must be able to concentrate totally on the task and have the ability to run through discomfort. It is the mental side of racing. . . . The tough competitor is the one who can push through the discomfort. A person who has the ability to put up with more pain than their competitors. All other things being equal it is this person who will win the race.*

Okay, fine, but how does one push through this darn discomfort? Is pushing through the discomfort a genetic trait? Can it be learned? Was it that I was trying to go faster than my training and conditioning would allow? Writing in *Sports Medicine for the Mature Athlete*, Albert Carron, a sport psychologist, suggests that motivation may be "the single most important factor influencing the performance effectiveness of the masters athlete." But knowing that motivation is important and applying it in a race is quite different. I was motivated but that wasn't helping me in the middle part of the race. I would start off the first mile at a solid pace and then around mile 2 my legs would begin to get that rubbery feeling. Or I'd lose concentration, start looking at my watch, and give in to the pain by backing off my pace. I slowed down, of course, to avoid the pain. This strategy didn't work because the pain was still there *and* I was running slower—it was a feeling that I was sinking into the concrete. In attempting to avoid the pain, I wasn't avoiding it at all. In fact, it was worse because the physical pain was still there and then I had to deal with my mental and emotional post-race pain associated with a poor performance. I let this observation fester for awhile as I wasn't sure what to do with it.

After a while, I realized that I couldn't push through the race discomfort until I embraced the pain in the middle of the race. I began to mess around with the pain doing 800 or 1200 intervals with the women's team on the x-country course. Whenever I started to experience weary or heavy legs (usually up hills), I tried to use that pain as a cue to pick it up a notch—to actually run faster. Doug suggested that I focus on a feeling of gaining energy from the ground to help me get more springy. The pain and heaviness in the legs needed to be positive cues that it was time to be a racer. So I concentrated on the pain; I embraced it. By embracing the pain I was beginning to bust through to the other side of expressing myself via the feel of speed, power, push, challenge. I could only experience these if I embraced the discomfort and then pushed through it. I needed the pain to experience the feel I wanted. Pain was a good thing. I had to embrace the pain because it was a big part of helping me push through to the self-expressive feel I wanted to experience. At the beginning of the fall I finally experienced this feel in a race.

9
THE FEEL

It was around the 2-mile mark of a 5K race in Loveland, Ohio that I spotted them: a pack of four runners—two women and a guy close together with another female runner a few strides behind the trio. I had seen them earlier in the race, lost sight of them, and now there they were. As I came abreast of the trailing woman, I could see she was struggling. "C'mon, you can catch them," I said. "That's what I'm going to do." My legs were beginning to get that heavy feeling, just as they always did at about this point in my races. But this time I was ready. I embraced the discomfort by relaxing as best I could. *Keep the form*, I reminded myself. Then I pumped the arms more quickly—the legs have to turn over faster—and kept my eyes glued on the pack in front of me. I was gaining ground. I was embracing the pain. Rather than just surviving, I was racing. I passed two of the pack at the 3-mile mark and used that as a sign to begin a kick. I had a little left, but so did the woman who had broken away from the other two. Her lead was too big to overcome (I found out later that she was the overall women's winner) and I finished a few seconds behind at 20:15. Although the time was my fastest in about 5 years, I was more pleased with how I felt during the race. I had done what Dave Scott, six-time Ironman Hawaii Champion, says he does, "During a race, I never wear a wristwatch, and my bike doesn't have a speedometer. They're distractions. All I work on is finding a rhythm that feels strong and sticking to it." My pace was steady throughout the race, about 6:30 per mile; I had embraced the mid-race discomfort and then pushed past it.

I had finally broken through and experienced the feel that drew me to this quest in the first place: strength, power, rhythm, and speed. Now that I felt the speed, I wanted more of it. This desire—whether good or bad—got me interested in what science had to say about running speed and training to get faster. I had no formal competitive running training in high school or college so I didn't really know much. Coach Ceronie introduced me to threshold and tempo runs, neuromuscular workouts, and different kinds of interval training, and I read about stride frequency and turnover, form, and running economy. But after nearly one year, I still didn't know much about the physiological principles underlying these training techniques. Maybe that's for the best.

Of course, when I refer to the need for speed, I'm not talking about all-out sprinting. To improve in the mile and 5K, I read somewhere that you need both speed and endurance. With knees that only a mother could love, my strategy was to focus primarily on building speed with shorter runs and interval work and secondarily on building up my endurance with longer runs. It seemed to make sense: most experts agree that the rate of decline of the fast twitch muscle fibers is much greater than the decline in our slow twitch fibers. Muscle sarcopenia—loss of muscle mass—is due to the age-related death of motor nerves and the loss of muscle fibers, mostly those fast-twitch fibers (Type II). The picture is not pretty if you want to gain, or even just maintain, speed as you get older.

As we age most of us have a much better chance of maintaining our endurance than our speed. No wonder many runners gravitate toward the longer, slower events—endurance capacity changes less than maximal muscle strength and power. You're much more likely to find older athletes competing at comparable levels with younger athletes in long distances events such as a marathon than in a 100-meter sprint. A study in the *Journal of Applied Physiology* found that endurance runners had a significantly greater proportion of Type I muscle fibers than when they were 20 years younger. Holding on to the fast-twitch fiber capabilities seems to be the challenge. Lactic acid is cleared by the fast twitch muscle fibers, so it's not too surprising that my legs felt heavy during those summer races. My muscles probably hadn't yet adapted to some of my training and my tolerance of the lactic acid was low—both physiologically and psychologically.

Shortly after my awakening in Loveland, I stumbled on the movie "Prefontaine" during some late-night channel surfing while half dozing in my Letterman-watching easy chair. I was mesmerized by the story. In my trance-like state, I saw myself with Pre on the University of Oregon track. I dreamed of running big. Then I woke up and went to bed laughing at the audacity of my dreams. Pre just wouldn't go away. That was twice now that he had appeared—the first had been when I was in my hives-induced, epinephrine stupor. Pre seemed to show up whenever I was in an altered state.

My infatuation with speed wouldn't go away either. I was finding that doing intervals or threshold type runs on the track or down at the cinders was by far my most engaging running activity—it was when I felt most alive. I loved the feel of running fast for a short distance, not all out speed but fast. This wasn't too surprising as in my pre-nonathletic life, I was the leadoff hitter, the point guard, the striker. I thrived in anything that involved quickness and anticipation (such as stealing a base). I didn't have blazing speed but I was quick. And the Miami women runners were beginning to accept me as an athlete. In our runs around the track, I would hear, "Way to go ladies . . . and you too, Dr. Jay." I was creating my own identity. And the track was becoming my sanctuary, that sacred place that gives you the peaceful feeling in the eye of life's storm. Yes, that *sacred place*. Joseph Campbell called it one's "bliss station." He writes,

> *This is an absolute necessity for anybody today. You must have a room, or a certain hour or so a day, where you don't know what was in the newspapers that morning, you don't know who your friends are, you don't know what you owe anybody, you don't know what anybody owes you. This is a place where you can experience and bring forth what you are and what you might be. This is the place of creative incubation. At first, you may find that nothing happens there. But if you have a sacred place and use it, something eventually will happen.*

I never suspected when I started the become-an-athlete quest that the track would be the thing to grab me, but it had. The track was becoming my sacred place, my bliss station. Now I had to figure out what to do with it. I grew an oval goatee as way to remind me of the feel I experienced on the track. My family didn't know quite what to make of it. Neither did I.

Around this time, I was in Daytona, Florida with my family on a business/pleasure trip and took my son to the Daytona USA Interactive Museum. Colin's favorite activity was driving (crashing) a simulated race car. Mine was a movie called Acceleration Alley, which depicted the life of auto racing. One of the racers interviewed said, "When I sit in the car, I feel like I'm home." Bingo! Being an athlete is about knowing how you want to feel and then placing yourself in physical situations where you can experience that feel as often as possible. Many high level performers talk about this engaged feeling. Malcolm Gladwell writes about hockey legend Wayne Gretzky in *The New Yorker*: "But what he [Gretzky] had was what the physical genius must have before any of the other layers of expertise fall into place: he had stumbled onto the one thing that, on some profound aesthetic level, made him happy." Of course, identifying this kind of feel for yourself doesn't mean you'll "be like Mike" or Gretzky but it is the only way to sustain something fulfilling over time and it's the best way to tap into your potential.

10
EASY SPEED

A little boy with straight brown hair and scrawny limbs jumped into a small swimming pool and splashed away from the edge. He couldn't even make it to the other side successfully, but the ripples of the water surrounding him were refreshing and inspiring. Even though he couldn't swim the length of the pool on his first try, he wanted to, and he knew someday he would get there. It wasn't long at all before Jeff Rouse reached beyond the length of the pool, and swam into a well of success. Jeff continued to explore the feel of his body gliding through the water as he pursued his love for swimming. He was very fortunate to have the support of his family and coaches as he continued on his nautical exploration.

Eventually Jeff was able to align his goal, to swim the length of the pool, with his Dream of being in the water, together through racing. From the time that he started racing he started linking the way he performed with the way that he felt. Whenever he finished a competition the very first thing his parents would ask him was, "How did it feel?" Later, his coach in high school and his swimming coach at Stanford University always asked this same question, "How did it feel?" Jeff was able to connect that when he swam his best, he felt his best. He noticed a correlation between the way he felt during the race, the way he felt after the race, and where he placed. During the races he felt engaged he also felt energized afterwards. Even more interesting is that the greater the engagement he felt, the better his time. Conversely, when he was disengaged during his performance he would feel drained afterwards, and these races correlated with poorer times.

Even though Jeff knew that there was a connection between the way he felt in a race and the performance itself, he didn't realize that he had any control over when that feel could occur. He always thought his best races happened by chance, and that he got lucky because they happened more often then they didn't. Going into the 1992 Olympics Jeff was the world record holder and the overwhelming favorite in the 100-meter backstroke. Jeff was

prepared for the 1992 Olympics to be the race where he would end his swimming career; he planned to leave the sport in glory. Jeff was prepared to put it
all out there, and then leave it in Barcelona.

Jeff had swum his entire life because it was something he loved to do; he
loved the way he felt and he happened to be great at it. He had always listened
to himself, to his family, and his coaches and they always associated his performance with a feeling he liked to have. And when he did this – he succeeded.
Before the Olympic games, he began to listen to new voices. Voices that told
him this would have to be the race of his life. Voices that told him no matter
how much he had accomplished in swimming he was nothing until he won the
gold medal. Jeff was listening to too many other voices, and worse, he began
to believe them. He began to believe that if he didn't win the Gold all of his
years in the sport were for nothing.

Jeff took his place in the third lane and was confident that he was about
to win the race of his life as he told himself, "It's just another swim meet, Jeff."
With a sudden blast above the crowd's cheers the gun went off and the swimmers went too. Jeff was notorious for breaking free of the group as they arose
for their first breath. This night he stayed true to his M.O. and started out
with the lead. As he surfaced, Jeff thought to himself, *Wow, I'm really here*,
and he took it all in as he plunged each arm over his head, pulling himself
through the water. Coming off the turn Jeff was still in the lead. It was just
a matter of holding on and he would prove that he really was something in
the swimming world. Five meters left to go and it looked like Jeff would be
taking home the Gold, but something didn't feel right. Jeff knew that he was
losing energy with each stroke and kick. What he didn't know was that in the
lane right next to him, Mark Tewksbury of Canada was gaining energy with
each pulse through the water. In the last strokes, with milliseconds between
them, Tewksbury managed to slip past Jeff and win the gold medal by six one
hundredths of a second.

If it hadn't been for the silver medal, Jeff never would have realized that
he could create his own feel as an athlete and as a performer. Jeff met Doug
and it couldn't have been more perfect timing for both of them. They sat
down together and started to talk. Jeff was able to describe *Easy Speed*, which
he considered to be a feeling of harmony with the water. When he felt his
best was when he felt he was swimming to 100% of his ability with only 80%
effort. He felt so engaged in what he was doing that he was gaining energy
while doing it.

Jeff knew that this was how he felt after a race he won, after a race that he
did great in. But he argued with Doug that this was not something he could
create. Jeff believed it was something that happened by accident. Fortunately,
Doug won the argument. The reality was that Jeff could train for Easy Speed.
He could train to feel the way he wanted to feel in the water. He would have
to practice by preparing. He engaged in the feel he liked to have and learned

how to create it. He did this for four more years. When Jeff went to the 1996 Olympics in Atlanta, he was committed to Easy Speed. He had prepared instead of practiced and he was there to feel the way he wanted to feel. Jeff had embraced his obstacle and learned from it. When he swam that race he felt Easy Speed, and all his preparing had paid off in the form of a gold medal and the feel he liked to have.

What I was discovering is that it's never too late to uncover and live this engaged feel of an athlete. If you are paying attention, clues to becoming the athlete you could, should, or want to be are all over the place. One day after a particularly trying work day, I was scheduled to do some intervals on the track with the x-country team. The rain was coming down in sheets as we were dealing with the remnants of a hurricane that barreled up the East Coast. It was windy, rainy, cold. I was tired. I changed into my running gear in my office and as I drove down to the track I almost turned around to head home. But something compelled me to keep going. At first, I didn't see anyone on the track. Then I spotted the Miami runners in their red practice gear jogging from the locker room to the track. I got this sense of being carried away by a sea of red. I had a vision of a parting of the Red Sea. My van drove through the storm into the calmness. I had this inner feeling that I was doing the right thing. Of course, I was soaking wet from the car to the track but the rain and wind seemed inconsequential. I had a higher purpose—to run and feel alive. As we did our 8 x 800s in the driving rain, the pounding of our feet on the track sounded like a herd of wild horses running free across the plains. When you know how you want to feel, it's amazing what you'll put up with to get it.

Age isn't a factor in knowing how you want your mind and body to feel. It doesn't matter if you are an elite, young Olympian like Jeff, a middle-of-the-road boomer such as myself, or a mathematics professor such as Marie-Louise Michelsohn.

11
THE FEEL WAKES UP
AFTER FORTY YEARS

Marie-Louise is running fast, real fast. She's running the mile course at Camp Taconic in the Berkshire Mountains. She gets up early every morning to time herself in the mile. She loves the feeling of running fast and soon is running 5:15 and then five minutes flat. Now it's time for the mile race, the culminating event at the camp each summer. But Marie-Louise can't run, not because she's hurt or slept in. The race is only open to the boys at the camp. Girls stay on the sidelines and cheer. It is 1953 and that's just the way things are. Girls don't run "long" distances.

"I was really mad," recalls Marie-Louise, who was 11 years old at the time. "I didn't understand why girls could not run in this race, especially since I had been running the distance all summer. After the race I checked the winning time and my time would have won. That made me even madder."

After that experience, Marie-Louise forgot about her passion to run for a long, long time. There was school and other "girl" things to do. Her advisor in high school told her to avoid the physical education classes because her future was in math. Her advisor was partially right in that Marie-Louise earned her Ph.D. in mathematics and went on to be a professor at the State University of New York in Stony Brook.

Although Marie-Louise didn't know it at the time, she also had a future as an athlete. But it took more than 40 years for Marie-Louise to rediscover her passion and ability for running fast. But when she did, WHAM, BOOM, BAM! In June 2001, at age 59, she set a single age world record for the mile. In September 2001, she placed third in the Fifth Avenue Mile in New York, in the masters division (40 and older) in a personal-best time of 5:45.5. In the same race the previous year she had run a 6:10.8. These performances are quite amazing at any age but particularly incredible when you discover that

Marie-Louise didn't run again until she was 53.

Marie-Louise played a little bit of tennis in her late 20s and early 30s but didn't like the one-on-one competition. "I had a friend who I was a little better than and I couldn't stand it when I would get ahead in a match," she says. "It made me feel guilty because I knew she was feeling bad. Other than tennis, I was inactive most of the time."

But in 1995 Marie-Louise began to run to cope with the stress she was experiencing from helping her daughter recover from a life-threatening brain hemorrhage. "I was a wreck," she says. "I couldn't focus. I couldn't do anything. My niece was very worried about me and suggested that I take up running."

Ironically, her first run was about one mile and then she slowly increased the distance each week until she was up to about three miles at a time. Running helped with the stress so much that she just kept it going. Then she found out about a local, five-mile race only three weeks after her first run.

She recalls: "A neighbor of mine said, 'you are crazy to do that race for your first race. It has all kinds of hills.' But I did it anyway and I placed third in my age group. I was hooked after that but it's a very funny thing that hooked me. I lined up at the front with all of the fast runners; I just liked the idea of being at the front. Everyone said, 'No, it's too fast for you, blah, blah, blah. You'll get killed.' Then I went out and all of these runners naturally passed me. And I loved that. I loved the energy; I loved that feeling of this wave of people coming by me with all this energy. Then at a certain point, you get into a group that runs your speed. But I loved all the energy, and I still do. I love all the energy during and after a race."

At the age of 53, Marie-Louise was hooked on running because of the stress relief, an age-group award, and the energy related to being passed in her first race. Not what we typically hear about birth-of-a-champion experiences.

After that race, Marie-Louise's competitive fire was born again. "I am very competitive but in a fun way," she says. "I was competitive within myself initially, setting this thing of trying to go a little longer each week. After a while I was timing myself. Yeah, pretty quickly I was timing myself. I like the competitiveness of running more than tennis. It's not like I'm trying to beat this person or that person. I'm trying to beat myself."

So how did she get so good in only a few years time?

"I actually started to get faster and faster pretty quickly," she says. "I think it's partly because I started to hang out with this group of runners who were members of a track club. They seemed to have fun and were very positive. That's what this is all about anyway. It's why I do it. It's just plain fun."

Marie-Louise still thinks she can get faster but even if she doesn't she likes the person she has become since she began running. "I think of my running as creating a whole new life for myself," she says. "It's incredible to be doing something new and succeeding at it later in life. It gives you a certain youth. It's very funny. When I run in races, I'm very often running next to women who are 29 or something like that. I look at them; I don't look in the mirror very much. I've never been much of a person to look in the mirror. I just look around me, and the people around me are much younger than me so I feel like I'm the same age. There's kind of an identity confusion. There's a part of me that knows I'm much older, but there's a part of me that feels like I'm 29. I feel I have more energy than I have ever had and I'm more fit than I ever was."

There's work involved, of course, but ultimately Marie-Louise runs for the pure joy of running. "You do have to really work hard at it," she says," but I love the work. In a way it's not work. I just love it. This is what I always say to people about exercise and doing athletic things, 'Find a thing you love to do because you won't do it unless you love to do it.'"

The passion play continues for Marie-Louise since I interviewed her a few years ago. In 2007, she "peaked" and set eight world indoor and outdoor records in various events in the 65-69 age group, although a couple of those records were subsequently broken by other competitors. And she does continue to run faster. At 66, she posted a new W65 world indoor 1,500-meter record with a time of 5:52.1, a full five seconds faster than her record set at 65.

12
BREAKTHROUGH AT THE BREWERY

One day at practice, Coach Ceronie said, "You should do a mile trial on the track to see where you're at. I think the men's team is doing one tomorrow. "Uh, sure," I said. I showed up at the track the next day not sure what to expect. I had never done a mile on the track with other runners. As I warmed up, a couple of throwers on the team were running an 800 (I never did ask why they were doing an 800 time trial). These guys were big and the whole team was cheering them on (while laughing) as they rumbled to the finish line. They finished gut and gut and then both crumbled to the ground as if they had been imploded. It reminded me of a race that took place many years ago at the village ballpark in my hometown. As my dad tells it, two big local guys got involved in an argument over who was faster. This discussion came to a head during the break of a Sunday doubleheader between my dad's town baseball team and a team from the next town over. As I understand it, the betting was fast and furious and it was decided that the race would be from home plate to first base. Someone had the sense to capture this athletic highlight on film and in the picture it shows both runners shirtless with their bellies hanging over their belts. I remember watching this race with my brother laughing along with everyone else. But the photo shows two determined 300-pound plus runners. I suppose the amount of money at stake may have had something to do with the seriousness of their expression. But racing does seem to get people serious.

I lined up with about 10 or 12 other runners and then we were off. The time trial was over before I knew what had happened. My goal was 5:40 and I finished in 5:33. I was quite ecstatic. I started doing the math in my head: *Let's see my fastest mile was 5:06. That's 27 seconds divided by four. That's only seven seconds per lap that I need to speed up to be as fast as I was 14 years ago.* The athlete mind doesn't see reality. We see what might be possible. And we don't think age is a factor even though it is. I was thinking it was possible to get even faster.

A few weeks later, I was in the tiny town of Trenton lined up on the starting line of a Sunday afternoon 5K that looped around the Miller Brewery (Ironically, I had given up alcohol a few years ago when I read that it could cause arrhythmia, which I had been experiencing). I had run this event two years ago when I was a dabbler and remembered the flatness of the course.

The fall air was cool as about 100 of us pain seekers left the starting line. As we reached the first mile, I heard "5:56," which prompted me to say, "Oh no, too fast." The guy running with me said, "don't let up. It's flat. You can keep the pace." So I dug in. I embraced the pain and pushed past it. We took turns passing each other and blew by some young kids, which pleased me no end. At two miles, I was at 12:11. "Geez," I muttered, "I can do this." At the third mile, I was at 18:30 and then I just went, finishing in 19:09. I shattered my expectations. If this is what they call a breakthrough, I just had one. My time was two minutes faster than two years ago.

I hung around afterwards and listened mindlessly to the post-race awards being doled out. And then I heard my name being called as the first male master runner. I had no idea they even gave out awards for first-place masters runners—anyone 40 and over. I didn't win any beer—fortunately—but liked the photo/plaque I received. Out of respect, I hung around for the remainder of the awards ceremony. The wheelchair winner, a young girl, received the loudest applause and she had a smile that just wouldn't quit. As I headed to the car, I looked back and saw the wheelchair girl still smiling. I thought of my own kids and how lucky I was. I cried silent tears most of the drive home trying to understand the way of the athlete with my award staring at me in the passenger seat. Was I being selfish for pursuing something that in the bigger picture of life was somewhat meaningless? Or was there really something to the way of the athlete? I didn't have an answer.

13

I AM SUPERMAN
AND I CAN DO ANYTHING

"Now what?" Coach Ceronie asked. We were in his office a few weeks after my peak performance in the Trenton race. I was surrounded by pictures of former Miami women runners—all of them champions of some kind—up on Coach's wall. There was that champions wall again just like at the physical therapy office. I was never quite good enough to be up on someone else's wall. That just gnaws at me. *I'd like to be up on a wall somewhere. I'd like to be a pinup guy.*

"I don't really know," I said. "I just want to keep feeling the push, the speed, the rhythm."

"But don't you have a goal of some kind." Spoken like a coach.

"Well, I do like the shorter distances. I'm kind of thinking I want to do something on the track," I blurted out.

"There's an indoor invitational meet in Indianapolis that we're going to in January. Why don't you run the mile?"

"You mean anyone can run?"

"Yep."

"But I'll get killed by these college studs. I'll get lapped. I'll look like a fool."

"Naw, they put you into heats according to pre-meet times. You'll be okay. Let me know and I'll sign you up."

"Okay," I said without thinking too much more about it.

I ran three more 5K races in late fall, culminating with the Polar Express and the Jingle Bell Run for Arthritis on back-to-back weekends in early December. The Saturday night before the Polar race, while watching the news with my wife, cold and snow were predicted. "Maybe you shouldn't go," Kim said. "It's going to be nasty." I wanted to run in the race to compare to last year's time. But I would also have to wake at 6:00 a.m. and drive an hour in in-clement weather. "I'll think about it," I said. Just before going to bed, I pulled out my stash of inspirational stuff. I knew what I was looking for. Found it. **"Polar Bear Tracks*"—John J. Kimiecik, Second place.** In the poem, written by my father and placing second in a local competition, a man and his dog experience normal, everyday winter tasks, such as shoveling snow, as harrow-ing, life-threatening events. The poem begins, *"I never shovel snow as ordinary men do. . . . "* I usually cut to the chase and read the last stanza:

> *My wife, a silent witness from the warmth and safety*
> *Of the bay window,*
> *Has never sensed our dangers—applauded our heroism . . .*
> *But just today, before we plunged through*
> *The storm door,*
> *Into the blinding snow to the bird feeder,*
> *(following safety lines, of course)*
> *she faced me squarely, snugged up the hood of my parka,*
>   *and whispered misty-eyed,*
>   *"Please be careful . . . I saw polar bear tracks*
>   *on the patio*
>   *this*
>   *morning."*

*Because young boys waiting on the bench to pinchhit for their big league
hero are not the only ones to dream.

My father still lives in the same small New York town in which he was born and raised. He was an excellent athlete, and my brother and I got at least some of his sports genes. Playing sports was his life for many years and so growing up it was ours too.

Baseball was our family's lifeblood, especially in the summer. Dad was our small town's baseball guru. For years he coached these semipro teams that were the best in the region. My brother and I practiced with the teams, we kept score, and we helped take care of the field. Sundays started out with 9'oclock mass. Then we would go with dad to the ball field. We drove the trac-tor and dragged the field. We lined the field and the batter's box. There was no better feeling than looking at the ball field we had prepared for the game later that afternoon. Then we would stop off to visit with Whitey Kowalcyck, the old-timer. My brother and I would play whiffleball with his sons while my dad and Whitey talked baseball. Then it was time for lunch at Grandma Golembowski's house and on to the game. Sometimes dad would let us take batting practice with the team. As batboys, we even got to wear miniature team uniforms.

Sometimes we had long road trips to play teams up north in cities such as Kingston and Poughkeepsie. I loved going on those trips. These bigger city teams couldn't beat us and hated us because we were so good. I don't know why my dad's teams were so good. But all of the local greats wanted to play for him. One memory I have is going to an off-season coaches' meeting with my dad when I was in seventh grade. I brought along my science book to study because I had an exam the next day. I was so excited to get to go to a meeting with dad. I was a big shot. I didn't study much as I found eavesdropping on the meeting much more educational—lots of smoke and swearing. On the drive home, we hit dense fog. My dad told me to help him by keeping my eye on the white line that separated the road from the shoulder. I can remember feeling scared but also feeling important.

Lots of great memories with dad but the most vivid one I have is playing catch with him in our backyard. I don't remember him ever saying no when I asked to play catch, and I asked often. He would throw me fly balls, ground balls. He'd let me pretend I was Tom Seaver, the great pitcher for the New York Mets. I was always a flawless pitcher when dad was the catcher. I would strike out almost every batter. I pitched perfect games. We would play catch until mom called us in for dinner. Then he would put his arm around me and say something like, "Great game, Tom. You really had your stuff today."

Dad is going to need his best stuff over the next few years. The diagnosis of multiple myeloma, a rare form of bone-marrow cancer, came a few years ago. I remember the Spring day my mom called me at work with the news. When we arrived home after I picked up the kids from their after-school childcare, I instinctively asked Colin if he wanted to have a catch (he was usually the one doing the asking so it didn't take him long to say yes).

"Throw me the ball, dad." I heard Colin say.

I looked at the ball in my hand and then at my son. "Sorry," I say. "Here you go."

"Are you ready, Dad?"

"I sure am, Colin." I crouched into the catcher's position. "Who you going to be today?"

"I'm Roger Clemens of the New York Yankees," he said with a gleam in his eye. I smiled at the irony of the situation. Grandpa Kimiecik was a die-hard Brooklyn Dodgers fan who transformed to a Mets fan when the Dodgers bolted for LA. He despises the Yankees and Colin knows it.

Colin let it fly. "Strike one," I shouted. It's simple, really. Fathers playing catch with sons. I hope my son remembers.

Misty-eyed I folded Dad's tattered and torn poem and stuffed it back into my emotional stash. I don't shovel snow as ordinary men do. I was going to that race. *That's a first-place poem, Dad.*

Sunday morning was cold but not as snowy as the weekend weather geek had predicted. The drive was uneventful and so was the race. I sloshed in at 19:52, about 45 seconds faster than the previous year. Not bad, considering the slippery conditions of the course and the cold. I rewarded myself with a cup of Dunkin Donuts decaf and a honey bran raisin muffin and headed back to Oxford. On the drive I thought about something Robert Redford had said when being interviewed on the Charlie Rose show. Rose had asked, "What one theme cuts across most of your movies?" Redford responded with "Heart. It is about looking for the heart." Somehow I knew that this quest to become an athlete was my way of finding my heart, my passion. I had lost it somewhere along the way. The athlete's way is not only about finding the magic for the first time or reconnecting with it, but also living it. And that's what racing does. It gives you the chance to experience it all—the pain, the pleasure, the push, the rhythm. The athlete finds the heart and then lives it out. The athlete has to race.

Six days later at the Jingle Bell Run in Northern Kentucky, I stood at the starting line with about 1,000 other runners searching for the heart. Amazingly, I recognized no one. I felt alone amid the mass of humanity. *The last race of the season, make it a good one*, I told myself. I blitzed the out and back course, which wound its way over and around the bowels of the city, finishing in 19:38. The race was a surreal experience. About halfway through, I heard, "GOOOOOOOOOOOOO, JAY." *Must be Amy*, I laughed to myself. *She's helped me look for heart over the years.* Then at about the 2.5 mile mark, while running up the final hill, I glanced to my right and saw a train going somewhere. Then I realized I was beating the train. I was running faster than the train! Faster than a locomotive. This blew me away. Lyrics from a song popped into my head: *I am Superman and I can do anything.* I kept repeating that one line as I busted up the hill. I released down the hill and headed for the chute waxing people right and left. A young girl—she couldn't have been more than 13—and I ended up side by side (the beauty of racing: age isn't a factor). Beauty nosed out age in this case and we congratulated each other while walking back to the convention center. Inside, I gulped down some chili, a banana, and a bagel. Everything seemed right with the world, except for my right knee, which was hurting like heck.

LAP 3
SLAYING DRAGONS

"The athlete who is in top form has a quiet place within himself, and it's around this, somehow, that his action occurs."
—Joseph Campbell

. . . This hurts so much, I want to quit. Why would anyone voluntarily succumb to this pain and torture? At least I'm not going to be lapped. Stay tall, stay strong, hold on. Stay with this guy. Maybe you can pass him on the last lap. My lungs are going to burst. Embrace the pain, Jay, embrace the pain.

At the end of lap three I was at 3:48. Another 76. Great job. *Three hundred meters to go and the pain is over. Hold on. I'm losing it. Help me, Pre. Help me, God. Someone help me . . .*

14
TESTING, TESTING

I wanted to have my knee checked out but the middle of December seemed to repeatedly slap me in the face—final exams, WHACK!, Kim's birthday, WHACK!, a new puppy, WHACK, WHACK!, a scheduled vasectomy (which I whimped out on at the last minute), WHEW! Staying true to my modus operandi, I delayed going to the orthopedic doc. Some of it was time; some of it was fear. I did at least visit our family physician who told me to rest and ice. Rest? Didn't he know I was racing against time.

I met with Luann to revisit my resistance training routine and to reassess my body composition. She gave me a new water routine, which mimicked the dry land intervals, but without the pounding. With my knee acting up, plunging back in the water seemed to be a good idea. Of course, I didn't try out the new routine until about a month later.

Back in spring I had undergone my first body fat assessment with an electronic impedance device in Luann's office as a quasi-baseline measure of my body's state of being. At that time, I weighed 160 pounds with about 12.3% body fat. Not bad, but certainly not a runner's profile for someone 5'8". The catalyst for getting my body composition assessed was a day when I looked in the mirror after a shower at the Rec Center. I didn't recognize the body staring back at me. With clothes on, I looked in shape; buck naked, I looked a little flabby around the midsection with love handles on each side. *I need to get leaner and meaner*, I thought. I had gained about 10-12 pounds over the past 15 years, which would certainly not help me in my attempts to run fast.

It was around this time that I started doing more intense interval work with the Miami women runners and a few longer runs of 5 miles or so each week. I retested in June without much change, and now here I was in December after a rigorous fall training regimen and racing schedule. In seven months I had lost nearly 10 pounds (down to 151) and registered 9% body fat. I was also much stronger as indicated by my jock-fixing performance on the strength tests.

My results aren't all that surprising. The interval work once or twice a week, combined with the core resistance training once or twice a week, was the key to my body transformation. I am much leaner and stronger than I was one year ago.

My friend Tony, a former competitive bodybuilder and Certified Strength and Conditioning Specialist, tried to explain my body transformation to me. He argues that a high-intensity, 20-minute interval workout utilizes an absolute larger percentage of calories over a 24-hour post-exercise period than does traditional aerobic exercise. His theory proposes that a higher metabolic rate and thermogenesis—higher body temperature—is attained through a 15-minute interval workout, which simply leads to greater fat burning over the long haul than going for an hour walk where you only burn fat during the exercise. Plus, the interval work—along with my resistance training—added lean tissue to my glutes, quads, calves, and hamstrings and more muscle means a higher metabolic requirement.

This whole idea of regular aerobic exercise, or, more recently, moderate-intensity physical activity that the experts tell us to build into our day just doesn't add up. People are getting fatter and one scientific report stated that we need 60 minutes a day of this kind of activity just to maintain our weight. I guarantee that anyone who performs six months of core resistance training twice a week, combined with one or two interval workouts, will get the same relative effects as I did: a leaner, meaner, weight loser. You don't need a best-selling lifestyle or fitness book to help you figure this out. These programs aren't anything special. For anyone who follows them, these kinds of programs probably work in the short term. But so would just about anything else if you stay with it. These programs don't work in the long haul because you can't adhere to someone else's program for the rest of your life. You have to pay attention to your own life and develop your own thing. You must create your own infrastructure on which to build your life. You can't do that by reading someone's book about how he or she did it and how you can to do it too.

What you need to do is to begin paying attention to how you want your life to feel. I wanted to become a fortysomething athlete because I paid attention to some clues that told me I would experience a feel I wasn't getting in my nonathletic life. I wasn't sure what feel exactly but that's kind of the fun part. I was becoming an athlete on my own terms, in my own way. Of course, I recruited people to help me along the way—as did Jeff Rouse and Marie-Louise Michelsohn—but I am making and breaking my own rules.

People who change and sustain anything are the ones who find a way to feel engaged in what they're doing. All of these programs claiming to have the fitness secret are just bells and whistles that distract you from getting engaged in moving and training your own body. They don't work in the long haul because they actually pull you away from paying attention to your performance process. As I stand on my soapbox all I can say is stop thinking the answer lies outside of you. Begin to listen to your little voice and make it bigger.

15

THE MUSCLES AT THE HEART OF IT ALL

The day after my office visit with Luann, I was on the road to Columbus, Ohio to undergo my second VO$_2$max test at Ohio State University. I had conned Steve Devor, an exercise physiologist and aging expert, and one of his doctoral students into measuring my maximum aerobic capacity at various points throughout the quest. I had barely survived a quasi-baseline VO$_2$max test in April. As I neared the end of my first pain and torture test back in the spring, I remember hearing "Keep going, Jay. You're doing great. You look good." I knew Dr. Devor and his trusty sidekick, Craig, were doing their best to motivate me to keep going—surely I didn't look good. Sweat was pouring down my forehead on to my glasses and the mouthpiece was full of saliva. I was near the end. My legs were wobbly and I felt my lungs were about to burst. I tried to keep going but a few seconds later gave the thumbs down, which was the predetermined signal to slow down the treadmill and put me out of my misery. I felt like such a wimp but they told me everyone feels that way after a VO$_2$max test—we all think we could have lasted just a bit longer.

David Costill, one of the research gurus on aging and physical performance, writes in *Running: The Athlete Within* that most exercise physiologists consider VO$_2$max—the maximal amount of oxygen that can be consumed by the body—to be the best single indicator of endurance potential. But from a pure performance perspective, VO$_2$max is not very good at predicting who is going to win a race as studies show that the runner with the highest VO$_2$max does not always cross the finish line first. This is one of the mysteries of human performance—VO$_2$max is a marker of endurance potential but many other factors influence how fast you can run in a race. Reading exercise physiology jargon usually turns me into a glassy-eyed moron. It's a science and a language that I just don't get but it seems so vital to performance that I have tried to educate myself.

If VO$_2$max isn't the key factor to peak performance, what is? One idea

from the literature suggests that the best runners are just darn good at resisting fatigue. Costill proposes that champion runners have a higher capacity for
tolerating high levels of stress than those who run in the middle or back of the
pack. Some of the elite runners tested in his lab over the years were able to run
for up to 30 minutes at 86% to 90% of their VO_2max. So even if your VO_2max
is less than other runners in your age group, you can still kick their butts—or
at least compete with them—if you can race at a greater percentage of your
VO_2max to make up the difference. Also, the runners that can tolerate up to
90% of their VO_2max seem to accumulate less lactic acid, which is a marker
of fatigue. Costill thinks this ability to resist fatigue has something to do with
muscular adaptations during training.

Tim Noakes, an exercise physiologist at the University of Cape Town
and Sports Science Institute of South Africa, believes that the Kenyans—
the greatest endurance runners in the world—have superior fatigue resistance
when compared to all other groups of runners. The results from one of the
studies in his lab showed that African runners had a higher resistance to fatigue when running at the same percentage of peak treadmill velocity as Caucasian runners, despite both groups having similar VO_2max values. And the
difference was astounding—the African runners' mean time was 98% longer
compared to the Caucasian runners. Basically, the African distance runners
can run at a higher percentage of their VO_2max than any other group of runners. Noakes proposes a number of possibilities to explain this phenomenal
resistance-to-fatigue ability but, like Costill, he zooms in on the muscles. His
data show that the skeletal muscles of the Kenyans during their high running
speeds of prolonged duration have an incredibly efficient oxidative capacity.

Now why are the skeletal muscles of the Kenyans so good at taking in
and using oxygen during a race? One guess from the experts is that the highly
efficient running form of the Kenyans—not their actual VO_2max—slows the
rate of rise of body temperature as well as the accumulation of metabolites in
the muscles that cause fatigue during training or a race. In fact, a high VO_2max
with poor running economy, according to Noakes, causes a more rapid rate
of heat accumulation and quicker onset of fatigue. It is not so much the heart
but the muscle that is at the center of peak running performance—the ability
to maintain a high percentage of your VO_2max throughout a race; the ability to resist fatigue. This notion seems to parallel my ongoing psychological
challenge to fight through race discomfort. Resisting fatigue in performance
situations seems to be based on a complex interplay among our physiological,
musculoskeletal, and psychological systems.

Noakes suggests that the reason why the Kenyan running form is perfectly
suited to middle and long distance is that their muscles act like springs during
exercise—Doug knew this intuitively when he suggested I focus on gaining
energy from the ground during my races. According to this biomechanical
model, the more the muscle acts like a spring, the less energy it consumes and

the more efficient it is. The more efficient, more elastic muscle will enhance performance by enabling you to run at a greater percentage of your VO_2max. So is the key to being a great distance runner having hyper springy muscles that have a killer capacity to utilize oxygen? If so, how could I get more spring in my step?

I called Peter Weyand, a former researcher at Harvard and now a professor at Baylor University, who has spent a lot of time studying the mechanics of running speed. It is partly his work to which Noakes was referring. Dr. Weyand was very patient and did his best to explain this spring idea since it was obvious I was in over my head. Dr. Weyand explained it this way: "If all other things are equal, the more you press on the ground the more you pop into the air and the more time you spend in the air. The faster people run the greater time they spend proportionally in the air. A good middle distance runner has the ability to apply high ground forces." This makes sense because the less force you apply, the longer your foot is on the ground. What's even more interesting is that the African runners in one of Noakes' studies had a lower percentage of slow twitch fibers than did the Caucasians. Noakes theorizes that the fast twitch fibers serve as important "power generators" at high running speeds. This leads me to believe that the African runners have a greater capability of applying high ground forces not only because of the efficiency of their running form but also because their muscles are acting as power generators. Add to this the superior oxidative capacity of their muscles and you have highly efficient runners.

I really didn't know what to do with this information. I tucked it away as a sign that things aren't always what they seem—paying attention to my musculoskeletal and neuromuscular systems was just as important as training the cardiovascular system to run faster at the middle distances. This point was highlighted by the results of a study in the *Journal of Applied Physiology* that examined the effects of explosive-strength training on 5K running times. One group of elite cross-country runners added in a 9-week program (about 30% of their total training) comprised of 20-100 meter repeats, jumping exercises, and leg press and knee extensor/flexor exercises with low loads but high or maximal movement velocities. A control group of similar ability runners just continued with their endurance training supplemented with some circuit training. After the program, the 5k times of the explosive-strength training group of runners were significantly faster than the control group. The authors suggest that the primary reason for the faster times in the explosive group were *neuromuscular adaptations* as no muscle hypertrophy took place.

All of this scientific work on the muscles' significant contribution to running performance seems even more relevant to us ageless athlete wannabes. The couple of long-term studies examining masters runners over many years as well as a few cross-sectional studies show that the very properties we want to develop in the muscles to run faster begin disappearing or go into hibernation as we get older. To run fast we need elastic, neurally fired-up, oxygen-charged muscles. The aging process is cruel in this regard. Dr. Auriel Forrester, a world-champion masters cyclist, explains that as we get older our connective tissue proteins, such as collagen, become more knotted and twisted like a grunge rocker's uncombed hair, which reduces our muscular elasticity—we're not as springy. The increasing rigidity of the collagen fibers also causes a decrease in strength of the connective tissues. If you are a runner and all you do is run, you are setting yourself up for less-than-optimal performances as you get into your 50s, 60s, and beyond. Costill's 22-year study shows that running does not maintain muscle mass. The older runners experienced a rather large increase in fat content with an equal loss in muscle content. The fast twitch fibers are the first to go. Costill writes,

> It is thought that slower movement and lack of explosive movement as we get older contributes to this preferential loss of fast-twitch fibers. If these fibers are not recruited (activated) for long periods of time, the body thinks they are not needed anymore and the stimulus to maintain these muscle fiber types is lost. Over time, these fast-twitch fibers gradually shrink up and die.

So if you want to slow the decline of your running performance or to get even faster as you get older, you not only need strength training but also explosive-strength training. Another 20-year follow-up study by the late Michael Pollock and his colleagues at the University of Florida backs this up as the group of seventy something runners that lost the least amount of muscle mass was the one that performed regular weight training.

To bring all of this back around to my initial interest—VO_2max—you need a good supply of muscle to take up oxygen during running. If you lose it, your VO_2max heads south even faster. VO_2max decreases about 10% per decade after the age of 25 for the general population. The good news is that for a masters athlete, the decrease is about half of that—5% per decade. Costill's masters runners had about a 12% decrease in 25 years. Walter Bortz, a physician and aging expert, presented an analysis of top performance in diverse athletic events over time in the *Journal of Gerontology*. His conclusion is that 0.5% per year is a basic biomarker of the aging process. That is, no matter what you do, you are going to lose about 5% per decade after age 30, whether it be VO_2max, cerebral metabolism, maximal pulse rate, or how fast your nails grow. Dr. Bortz projects that a sedentary individual after the age of 30 loses function at a rate of 2% per year. At age 65, this individual will have lost 70% of maximal vitality and the frailty barrier—the most prevalent factor for entering nursing homes—of 30% of maximal function will have been reached. For the masters athlete, who is only losing .5% per year, only 30% of maximal function will have been lost after 60 years (age 90). Athletes hold on to their vitality much longer and there's another aspect to this process that the research doesn't usually address.

Much of the scientific work on masters athletes examining declines in physiological, respiratory, and musculoskeletal systems has been conducted on older runners or athletes who were elite when younger. Most of us didn't max out on our VO_2max when we were in our 20s and 30s because we didn't train to the max. Some of us were experimenting with the effects of drugs on our minds and bodies, surviving college, getting jobs, and raising kids. Most of us don't know what we are capable of doing athletically. Perhaps this is better. We don't have half a century of top-level performance behind us to mess with our heads. Who cares if all of these systems decline at .5% per year? I can find my athletic self no matter the rate at which my body is falling apart.

After my first VO_2max test, Craig sat down and reviewed my results with me. I was pleasantly surprised by my maximum oxygen uptake of 56.9, which certainly is no threat to my dream buddy Pre's 84.4, but does place me in the low-end of the ballpark of some of the masters runners who have participated in the long-term scientific studies I've just described. Of course, these masters runners were in their 50s when initially tested—I've got about 5 years on them. The research on these masters runners shows that 20 years later (now in their 70s), the group that maintained rigorous endurance training lost the least in maximal oxygen uptake compared to groups of similar age runners that cut back markedly or completely stopped training. When I first arrived at Miami in the early 1990s, a graduate student had tested my VO_2max as part of his masters thesis research project. My VO_2max in that study was 55.9. Of course, it is always dangerous to compare tests that were probably conducted using different protocols. But still, this was encouraging performance news.

16
THEN AND NOW

The two-hour drive to Columbus gave me a lot of time to reflect. As usual, I was making the drive alone. Throughout this quest, I have found myself alone a lot. Driving to races—alone. Running in races—alone. In most of my races, it seems that my pace puts me in no man's land. I'm not with the speed demons in front; I'm not with the penguins in the back. I'm not even in the middle. I'm in nowhere land—alone. Training runs—alone. Weight training—alone. One of the few times I'm not alone is when I train with the women in red. There's something warped about the whole process when my peer group is college women runners any of whom could be my daughter. But being an athlete means living your life differently from the masses. I recall reading somewhere that Jerry Rice, the greatest wide receiver to ever play in the National Football League, said "it's what you do when people aren't watching that sets the great ones apart from everyone else" or something like that. There must be some truth to this because only a small part of an athlete's life is spent performing in heated competition with and in front of others. The rest of the time is spent training, preparing, practicing. So what you do with that time is probably as important as what you do in the competitions themselves. Love him or hate him, Bobby Knight, the winningest Division I men's college basketball coach of all time, once said something to the effect that, "Everyone wants to win, but not everyone wants to practice to win." So being an athlete must be somewhat a lonely endeavor because how many people are truly going to practice, practice, and practice some more? Not many (more on this idea in Chapter 23).

When I was younger, my brother practiced with me almost all the time. Well, actually he beat up on me most of the time but at least I wasn't alone. We rarely see each other now as we're 700 miles apart and even further apart in how we are living our lives. But growing up we were only 10 months apart biologically. We competed intensely. It was definitely a love-hate relationship, which most of the time seemed to be more hate than love. Being the younger brother, I always tried to live up to Greg's athletic prowess in all sports. We were even steven in most of them except for ice hockey. Greg was a very good skater, which put him in good stead with the hockey machos during the winter months when the sport ruled our small town. To put it bluntly, I sucked. I couldn't skate, could not handle the puck, and was about as tolerant of the cold weather as a Florida retiree. Because of this one weakness on my sports resume, I was moved to goalie for most games at the local pond—unbeknownst to my mother who had forbade me from serving as a punching bag for the big boys' missiles. I didn't mind being goalie as I was probably too young to realize how stupid it was. My brother and I would walk the mile to the pond together where he would shoot puck after puck at me. My equipment was comprised of baseball catcher's shin guards, my dad's umpiring chest protector, an old first-baseman's glove, kneepads, and boots in place of my skates to keep my feet warm. I looked more like a baseball catcher playing in Alaska than a hockey goalie. I got to the point that my quick reflexes and eye-hand coordination made me a decent defense against wrist shots and wrap arounds. My safety net was the "no slap shot" rule whenever I was in the goal, a rule that the older kids detested.

Paja, the local hockey stud, especially despised the rule. I remember in one game, he was breathing fire after I had stopped a few of his wristers. On a breakaway, he abruptly stopped, wound up, and let the slap shot fly. I tried to get my glove out in time to catch the puck but because of its speed misjudged. The puck smashed into my elbow and adding insult to injury continued up to hit me squarely in my Adam's apple. I fell to the ice writhing in pain. "Where's the puck, where's the puck," I heard Paja scream. My brother rolled me over and there it was safe and sound. No goal.

"It's right here, Paja," I can remember Greg saying. "Jay stopped you cold. What were you thinking?"

"I lost my head," he replied, still fuming over being stuffed again by a neophyte goalie.

I wanted to say I was okay but I couldn't speak. Not that it mattered—there seemed to be more concern about the location of the puck than my physical condition. I played the rest of the game, masking the pain, and then everyone called it quits. We walked home basking in the afterglow of my performance. Greg was going on and on about what a great stop I had made. "Do you realize how fast Paja's slap shot is?" he asked. All I could do was shake my head. "Well, it's fast, it's like Bobby Hull fast." Big brother was proud and that was enough for me. We trudged the rest of the way home together in silence.

Dr. Devor and Craig were waiting for me when I arrived at the Physical Education Building on OSU's campus. After another grueling bout on the treadmill, my VO_2max had increased three points to 59.6. This time I wasn't surprised. I knew even before testing that I had undergone a significant training effect during the summer and fall. And I knew by my performance in races that my systems were functioning at a high level. I had experienced the training effect. Felt good! They patted me on the back and sent me back to Oxford—alone again with my right knee crying for some tender loving care although I knew what I would get instead was more Pain and Torture.

17

BACK IN THE REHAB SADDLE AGAIN

Over the holidays I bit the bullet and finally made an appointment to see my orthopedist, who wasn't available until early January. What diagnosis would the New Year bring? I tried to get my story straight in my head so that the doc wouldn't catch on to my stupidity, which I knew was the reason for the knee pain.

"Man, that is one of the ugliest kneecaps I've ever seen," said the doc.

"Thank you, I'm quite proud of it," I replied.

It was a little more than a year after my first visit for patello-femoral dysfunction of the left knee. This time my right knee was the culprit. As the doc scrutinized my x-rays, I told him that my ugly kneecap was the result of a hairline fracture from my high school basketball days. It didn't heal properly and protrudes out on the lateral side. On the x-ray, it looked like I had two kneecaps—called "bipartite patellar variant" by the medical world.

I had been having some mild to moderate discomfort around the knee for about a month, especially after running. It wasn't going away—why would it, since I was dumb enough to keep doing things like VO_2max tests and intense interval work. Doc proceeded to poke, prod, and palpate his fingers all around my knee. He moved the knee this way and that and after what seemed like an eternally long time declared that "it feels like it could be plica syndrome."

Plica syndrome! "What the heck is a plica?" I asked.

"It's a little sac underneath a ligament on the medial side of the knee that can sometimes get irritated. When did you first notice the pain?"

"I'm not sure it just kind of came on." Of course, I didn't want to tell him what really happened but my Polish Roman-Catholic guilt got the best of me.

"Well . . . actually I ran a 5k race on a Sunday and then felt so like Superman the next day that I did a 3 x 1200, 1 x 800, and 1 x 600 on the track with the women's team. Then I ran another race the next weekend. After that race is when I really felt it." I didn't tell him about my out-of-mind Superman experience during the Jingle Bell race as I didn't think he would appreciate the metaphorical image.

"That wasn't very smart," he said.

Which part wasn't smart? Some of it or all of it?

"You were probably fatigued and when you did the intervals your body couldn't compensate the way it usually does, especially your knees. You over-did it."

No, really!

Before we start treatment for the plica, I want you to get an MRI to rule out the possibility of a meniscus tear. There's only a slight chance of that, but we can't really be sure until we see some pictures."

My injury experience is probably not much different from many boomers who are pushing the athletic envelope. In fact, the American Academy of Orthopedic Surgeons coined the term *boomeritis* to refer to the increase in older adult injuries. Most of this increase in injuries is due to those boom-ers exercising without training, such as weekend bicycle riding, basketball, and skiing. Most of the injuries that masters athletes do experience relate to overuse. In a study of older athletes over a 7-year period, 57% had sustained some injury that had limited their training for one or more weeks. In fact, rotator cuff injuries and complete tears, such as a knee meniscus, are much more common in athletes over 40 years of age. My quest experiences were so in line with the data that I could be an injury poster child for masters athletes. I could finally be up on someone's wall but for all the wrong reasons.

I scheduled my MRI for the next day at an imaging center in Cincinnati—more driving, more alone time. I very much doubted that I had a meniscus tear. But I didn't have another choice unless I wanted to hunt around for a different doc who would give me a referral to physical therapy without the MRI evaluation. That seemed to be more trouble than it was worth.

A week later I visited the doc again to review the MRI results, which stated: "Mild patellofemoral chondromalacia is present. No meniscal tear is identified. Moderate meniscal degeneration is identified."

"This is good news," the doc said after reading the report.

It is? What's this chondrowhatchyamacallit and musical degeneration?

"There's no tear of the meniscus. I think the main problem for you, Jay, continues to be the tracking of the patella, especially since you are doing some pretty intense running. Both knees seem to be susceptible. Your patella wants to go out and this pulls on ligaments on the medial side of your knee."

"What's your advice," I asked.

"Well, you need therapy to address your tracking problem and you should probably cut back on the hard surfaces."

I replied with my zinger.

"I've heard from a few of the Miami women runners that the other PT place in town has an underwater treadmill. Would that be something that could help me?"

"Sure, but they will probably start you on the patello-femoral protection program on dry land before you get in the water."

Good answer. I figured I might as well go for broke.

"Also, I was planning to run in this indoor track race in a few weeks. What's your thought on doing that?"

The doc just looked at me for what seemed like hours. In a way, I was kind of hoping he would say, "No way, no how. You should not run in that race. You will destroy your knee and all that goes along with it." This would have made it easy for me to bag it, to put me out of my mental misery, to succumb to the fear that was rising up like a New York City skyscraper. "Not the wisest choice," he replied, "but it's probably okay."

Darn.

Over the next 10 days I was in somewhat of a holding pattern, call it a forced taper, for the 1-mile race looming in Indianapolis. I tried calling to set up an appointment for PT but had to leave a message. They didn't call me back, which angered me at first. Then I realized that I oftentimes (okay, usually) don't call people back so I called again the next day. The earliest they could get me in was the day before the race. Fine, I said. In the meantime I kept busy by running on trails, doing my weight routine, and trying out the new water workout Luann had laid out for me. I was hoping that the busy work would squelch the fear percolating in my brain about the indoor race.

It was fun to be back in the water. I started by alternating between flutter and dolphin kicks. I held on to the side of the pool, extended out horizontally, and then kicked hard and fast for 30 seconds. After that came 4 sets of x-countries and jumping jacks. On each set, I started off easy then followed up with a drag motion, a jump, and a suspension, each of which is more difficult. I was in about 4 feet deep water so I wasn't wearing an aqua jog belt. I remembered Luann telling me that the goal for these exercises was to go high and hard. I tried to visualize a Randy Johnson fastball. That's what I wanted to be—a fastball up in the strike zone that even the best hitter couldn't hit. These kicked my butt. I surrendered to the pain.

On a Saturday morning one week before my indoor race I talked Colin into coming to the pool with me. I needed someone to motivate me through the pain. He was the likeliest victim as my wife had taken our daughter to the pediatrician for her annual checkup. As we got near the Rec Center, the vast numbers of cars and buses indicated a gigantic swim meet in progress. That's the double-edged sword of our Rec Center—it's such a wonderful facility that many swim meets are held there throughout the year. During these meets, parking is at a premium. I drove around a bit with no luck and said to Colin, "I think we'll just go home, son." Colin freaked out, "No, daddy, I have to coach you!" I couldn't pass that up so we finally found a spot and walked a good distance in the cold to the Rec Center. The foyer was packed with parents and swimmers in between events. Once we waded through the masses, the actual Rec Center wasn't crowded at all and there was no one in the leisure pool, except for the lifeguard. I explained to Colin what I was trying to do and, of course, he barraged me with questions, "Why are they called dolphin kicks? You don't look like a dolphin. What's a cross-country? Are you taking a trip?" As I began my routine, Colin turned into coach, "Go faster, daddy, you can do it. Don't stop." He did this a few times and then as expected got bored and started shooting baskets. I was alone again with the pain. When I finished up, we shot baskets together and I picked him up a few times so he could slam dunk. We raced each other a few lengths of the pool and then it was time to go. On the walk back to the car, Colin said, "That was fun." And it had been, simple fun between a father and son. I thanked Colin for helping me out. If he hadn't been with me, I probably would have ditched the workout.

Many times throughout this quest, I have wondered about the effects it might have on my kids. My fear initially was that the time spent on becoming an athlete might take away from time with the kids and family. There may be some of that going on but I've noticed that by working to get the athlete back into my life, my motivation to play with my kids has actually increased. My energy level seems elevated overall because I feel more like me. I feel better about myself and I think that gives me the energy to interact with my kids in positive, fun ways. Of course, this could all be just a way to rationalize how I'm spending my time.

I was finally able to get in to physical therapy the day before my first-ever indoor mile race. I greeted Mark, a giant of a man, who was the head of the physical therapy clinic. Mark had actually been a student in my graduate course quite a few years ago when he got his graduate degree in exercise science. He then went on to get his physical therapy degree and now here he was back in Oxford. He was another ex-college football player and physically intimidating. After sharing pleasantries, he got right into it, taking all kinds of measurements and asking me a slew of questions. He and a colleague had me walk back and forth so they could observe my gait. "Look at those legs," I heard them say. "He's an injury waiting to happen." I was used to these kinds of comments so I didn't say anything. As I understand it, the main problem I'm running into is a tendency for internal rotation of my upper leg, especially the left leg, combined with bow-leggedness. This structure causes internal rotation, which forces the patella to track out of its groove. Mark was a little concerned that the pain could be related to joint degeneration more so than irregular patellar tracking. He kept saying, "Well, if it's the joint line, there's not much we can do." I didn't think it was the joint line but hey what do I know. I told him about my race the next day and he asked me to mark with a pen where I experienced pain during and after the race. We would start in with more active PT next week. I walked out of there full of doubt about my future as a runner and I hadn't even started in with the Pain and Torture.

18
DESIRE GREATER THAN FEAR

That night the doubt about my ability to run the mile began to torment me. However, my desire to experience the feel of speed and push, which only racing seems to give me, was beginning to wash over me like a tropical waterfall. *Keep the desire greater than the fear.* To ease my fear and build my desire, I would periodically replay in my mind the "Prayer Pole" experience from a few months ago.

I was standing (more like shaking) about 40 feet up on what our outdoor adventure guide called the Prayer Pole. Scared out of my mind does not describe what I was feeling at that moment. The pole was part of a ropes course on the outskirts of Miami's campus and I had taken a class I was teaching out here as part of a group bonding experience. Truth be told, I just wanted to get us out of the classroom. Not much learning occurs in a college classroom. I don't know why college professors, administrators, and parents keep thinking that it does. The students know better. Deep down, I know I'd love to be uptown with them experiencing life rather than reading about it in some damn book.

Anyway, the idea was to climb up the pole (in a harness, of course), balance for a moment or two, and then leap outward to touch and ring a bell that was hanging a few feet away. None of the students volunteered to go first as I had hoped they would. I don't like heights—I get vertigo when I'm just standing on a chair changing a light bulb—but someone had to get it going. As the instructor, that responsibility fell to me. Here's the thing: the fear is not based on reality because you cannot fall with the harness on. Climbing up, however, is hard enough and then you have to jump out into space, out into the unknown. You just have to let yourself go and do it. You have to make yourself vulnerable. But the fear of falling is very strong. I barely made it to my balancing spot and then somehow I forced myself to jump. I missed the bell and then felt the harness tighten as the group gradually lowered me to the ground. A number of students then figured, "Well, heck, if our instructor had the guts, I might as well give it a try." Some of them reached the bell, which made me proud on the outside but pissed me off on the inside. A few of the students could not get themselves to do it. They succumbed to the fear. One even climbed to the top—on the precipice of success—only to climb back down, too afraid to jump out into the unknown. I decided to go a second time and I noticed the fear was much less intense. As I stood at the top of the pole, I shouted "Look, Ma, I'm on top of the world." Then I was out in the unknown and the sweet sound of the bell was music to my ears. I heard the cheers. I loved the feeling.

So the obstacle wasn't really the physical task, which wasn't that physically demanding. The real obstacle was the psychological fear—fear of falling, fear of heights. Everyone experiences this kind of fear in everyday life, maybe not as intense but fear just the same. But the good ones don't let the fear debilitate them. *They keep their desire greater than their fear.* That's why you really have to know how you want to feel about yourself and your life so that you don't run from the fear but meet it head on like a bull charging a matador's red cape. The feel you like to have builds your desire, which gets you through obstacles, such as fear and doubt. High quality performers know this and I was beginning to get it. You've got to pay attention to your feel and then figure out ways to experience and sustain it. That's the best way to put fear in its place.

19
MY LONGABERGER MILE

The morning of the mile race I was sitting in the stands with my wife and some other parents watching our daughter's basketball game. Somehow the discussion came up that I had to leave before the end of the game to drive the two hours to Indianapolis to run in a race. One of the parents commented, "You're driving to Indianapolis to run in a race that's only a mile?" The tone was one of incredulousness, which intonated something along the lines of "Why would you do such a thing, you stupid man?"

We then got into a discussion about men and women and how much freedom they have or don't have, blah blah blah. The point the women were making is that men have much more freedom to do their own thing—such as drive to Indianapolis to run in a meaningless race—than women do. This is hogwash at least from my perspective. I pretty much work all day and then cart the kids around to activities in the evening when Kim is on the road, which can be a few days per week. I don't go camping with the guys, I don't play basketball or golf on Sunday mornings, I don't go on wild man golf trips, and I don't drink or stay out late. In fact, these days the only thing I do outside of work and shuffling my kids around is train to be an athlete. This takes maybe 10 to 12 hours per week of my time, most of which is done on my lunch hour or late afternoon at the track. I was just thinking this stuff, I didn't actually say any of it. What I did say, finally, was, "Well, Kim does things that I could say the same thing about like when she went to that Longaberger basket place in Dresden with her Mom and Aunt. That was an all-day trip. So, if you think about it this race is just my Longaberger Mile." This, of course, was the wrong thing to say. The women just went off on me: "You can't compare the two! The trip to see how baskets are made was just a one-day special affair! It was a family bonding experience!" I wanted to come back with something like, *Yeah, but they're _ _ _ _ _ _ _ baskets*, but I didn't. I surrendered, kissed my wife and son, caught Carly's attention with a wave, and headed to Indianapolis.

During the drive, I had time to ponder the Longaberger Mile discussion. I'll admit that becoming an athlete in middle-age and beyond does require some selfishness. Again, maybe I'm just kidding myself, but I like Ken Pelletier's notion of "enlightened selfishness" that he writes about in *Sound Mind, Sound Body*. He found that individuals who were selfish about their lives—in the sense that they explored and lived for deep meaning and purpose—not only contributed more to society but also were also healthier than those who did not. To give credit where credit is due, Herbert Simon first coined the term "enlightened selfishness" in *Science* when writing about altruism and survival of the human species.

Enlightened selfishness, the good kind, is what I'm talking about. It is essential if you want to feel alive. And that's the whole point. If you're feeling alive, you'll bring other people alive, including your kids. Campbell comes to my rescue once again:

> *The influence of a vital person vitalizes, there's no doubt about it. The world without spirit is a wasteland. People have the notion of saving the world by shifting things around, changing the rules, and who's on top, and so forth. No, no! Any world is a valid world if it's alive. The thing to do is to bring life to it, and the only way to do that is to find in your own case where the life is and become alive yourself.*

It just so happens that for me to feel fully alive I needed to drive two hours to run in an indoor race. I think many parents believe the most important thing they can do to help their kids is to enroll them in activities and support them. The danger is that the parents then live a slow death while living through their kids. They yell and scream at refs, they strategize to get their kids in the right schools with the right teachers, and they buy them computers, TVs, and the latest technology. These parents invest much of their time in their kids, not themselves. They forget about the desire, the push, and the rhythm that being an athlete—or whatever is their bliss—can bring. Being an athlete shouldn't be wasted on the young. You really can't appreciate what your body can do or not do until you're in your 40s. Most of us give up on our bodies too soon and too easily. If you live your Dream—mine was to experience the feel of an athlete—your kids will be far better off than you living through them. You'll be more likely to transform yourself and the world in some positive way. My arguments always make sense when I'm in the car by myself. I cranked up John Mellencamp and barreled down I70 as my desire grappled for control of the looming Longaberger Mile.

In mythology, dragons symbolize obstacles a hero must overcome to experience transformation or rebirth of the self. Without facing and defeating the dragons, the hero will have nothing to bring back. But in Campbell's

Power of Myth, he proposes that the dragons are nothing more than symbols of our own inner demons. In essence, the dragons, or obstacles we face, are much more internal than external. It is how we respond to obstacles that separates the real athletes from the wannabes.

We all face obstacles to becoming what we believe in our hearts we could be. Maybe you are taking care of an ailing parent or maybe your partner isn't all that supportive of your ageless athlete ideas or maybe you have financial woes. External obstacles to finding your athletic self are very easy to find. I can't train today because: I need to get the kids to their activities, attend this very important meeting, the weather sucks, or an appointment with the eye doc is on the schedule. Becoming an athlete—or just getting out to exercise— is fraught with obstacles no matter the age. So how do some people overcome their obstacles and live out the athlete within, whereas others succumb to them? Simple: the performers know how they want their bodies to feel when in action, whether it be cycling, rowing, golfing, or playing tiddlywinks. And they make this feel so powerful and consuming that they'll go to any length to get it and sustain it over time. So my desire to experience what I believe is my destiny, my daimon, my magic, my bliss (take your pick) is driving me to Indy to run in what most people might label a "stupid" race. And this enlightened selfishness is a good thing as long as I also keep the athlete in perspective when looking at the bigger picture of my life with my wife and kids, my job, and my relationships. This is crucial, because if you don't create this powerful, internal feeling, what do you think you'll do when faced with obstacles? Give up, give in, watch from the sidelines, and succumb to the humdrum existence of everyday life.

The real barriers to becoming an athlete aren't the ones we hear the most about—age, health, injury, family, job—because we all have our own renditions of them. Now granted some people have real physical maladies that hamper their ability to do various sports. But for the most part, the real obstacles are what Campbell called the internal "dragon cage." We are all potential prisoners of our own dragon cage, which is full of self-doubt, fear, frustration, and guilt. As we get older, it might be more difficult to slay these internal dragons, especially if you weren't an athlete in your younger years. But they *can* be slain. Imagine the feel you like to have as your sword. You create the kind of sword you want by paying attention to the feel you want to experience in your life. As the feel grows, your sword becomes more powerful. It gets sharper and stronger and molded to fit who you are. Your sword needs to be unique to you because your dragons are different from mine. My sword will not help you defeat your dragons; you need your sword and I need mine.

I arrived at the race site—a gigantic, empty warehouse that housed the portable 200-meter track—an hour or so before my scheduled heat. I had never attended a college track meet before and was taken aback by the number of athletes sitting around doing nothing. I located the members of the Miami women's team many of whom were sprawled out on sleeping bags—some were reading, others were listening to music. I don't think I would have been a very good college track athlete. The waiting around would have driven me crazy. You might wait all day for your event and then, if you're a 100-meter hurdler, the race is over in a few seconds. Give me a basketball game where you arrive, you warm-up, you play a couple of hours, and you go home.

The warehouse and thinking about playing basketball reminded me of the summers of my youth when I worked in the onion fields for a local farmer. My hometown of Florida, New York—about 60 miles north of New York City—happens to be near a colossal swamp left over from the ice age that the immigrants from Poland, Ireland, and Germany converted to fertile, black-dirt farmland in the 1800s. Don't ask me why but black-dirt is very good for growing onions. There weren't many work opportunities for young kids in Florida so many of us ended up working along side the migrant workers for the onion farmers during the summer. It was brutal, dirty work and the hot sun made it worse. Out in the fields early and back in late. Depending on the work of the day, we were either weeding, pulling onions and topping them into crates at the ends of each field to make room for the harvester machine (for about 50 cents per crate), working on the harvester, or working in the barn screening the onions into 50 lb bags, sewing them up with needle and string, and then stacking them on pallets for storage. This is where my quickness got me in trouble. Even then I couldn't do anything slowly so I was taught to be a sewer and stack man—in my opinion the hardest god dam job in the entire operation. The bag man—usually my brother who took great pleasure in making me suffer—would hand me the bag and then in a matter of seconds I had to sew it up and stack it before the next 50 lb bag filled up. The only thing that kept me going besides the fear of Farmer Daegle's wrath was the hour we got for lunch. His oldest son—who by the way got to drive the forklift around—was a year younger than me and into basketball. That meant that the barn had a hoop. We would eat our bag lunch as fast as humanly possibly and then play hoops for about 45 minutes. We would come back to work drenched in sweat, energized for the four hours of hell that the afternoon would bring. We also played whiffleball in the barn at times. But whatever sport we played, that one hour was our sacred place, our bliss station. And now here I was in the sacred place of my adult athletic life—a track in a barn.

I had to keep reminding myself that I wasn't running with the women today and went to find out how to check in. Although the Stan Lyons Invitational (the official name) was open to any athlete, I didn't get the feeling that there were many runners my age hanging around the warehouse. I bumped into Coach Ceronie and he said they were running behind so I had about 90 minutes or so of waiting around. After paying my $10 entry fee, I checked the listings. I was in the fourth heat (the slowest group) for the men's mile. Seeing my name on the list seemed strange. I watched some of the action on the track. Energy just oozed from the center. Coaches were yelling at their runners to run faster, fans were cheering and clapping. And Andrea Kremer was running. One of the best middle-distance runners Miami has ever had, she was leading the women's 5,000 meter race. Andrea was making the other runners appear motionless as she lapped many of them into submission. I knew that soon I would get that feeling of being lapped. I've never experienced being lapped but it must be a helpless feeling. Here you are busting your ass when someone like Andrea comes whizzing by you. I pushed that thought out of my head and went to warm-up.

I watched the three men's mile heats before mine, trying to get an idea of what I had to do. A mile was 8 laps. My zealous goal was to run each lap at a 40 second pace to finish in 5:20. The winner of the first heat was a guy from Eastern Kentucky University with a time of 4:16. I tried to calculate on what lap I would be lapped but I got confused with the math. Then my heat was up. We lined up and the gun went off. Surprisingly I wasn't last. I passed a kid who had a beer belly and wondered why he was running. I made a mental note to ask him after the race but I never found him. The hardest part was getting a rhythm while surrounded by other runners. Now I can see how Mary Decker and Zola Budd crashed in the 1984 Olympics. One misstep and you're history. My first lap was 37 and I knew that was too fast. Second lap 40. Third lap 41. Fourth lap 42. I was right on target at 2:40, halfway to my 5:20. But I was slowing up. My last four laps were 43, 43, 45, and 44 for a 5:35 finishing time in my first-ever official indoor track race. Coach Ceronie tried yelling at me to run faster, something like, "C'mon you old man, get moving," and I heard the cheers from the Miami women runners, but my body did not respond. Those last four laps were survival. I don't even remember being lapped.

During my warm-down around the inside of the warehouse, I was approached by a runner wearing a Lindenwood University (St. Charles, Missouri, for those of you with geographical curiosity) racing singlet. Jake introduced himself as a runner who was in my heat and then asked how old I was. After he got over the shock, he asked, "Why did you run today?" I thought about the question for a second or two and said, "Because I love the feel." I said it kind of off the cuff but later realized it was the truth. If you can run, you should. If you want to be an athlete, you should. If you want to feel alive, you should. It is your responsibility to live out the Dream that is inside you. We exchanged pleasantries and wished each other the best with our running. He seemed like a good kid. I checked the online results later that night and lo and behold Jake had won our heat in 4:46. He had been one of the runners that lapped me. I packed up my gear, gave a few of the Miami women runners a wave, and left my sacred place, a place that I swear smelled like onions.

20
WAITING FOR SPRING

February and March were spent dealing with old man winter and Pain and Torture. I'm not sure which was worse. Running in the winter months around Southwest Ohio is always a crap shoot. This winter was particularly bad with more snow and ice storms than usual. As we all waited for Spring, I was waiting for a sign of some kind as to where I should go next with the quest. I decided to shoot for the Lou Cox Memorial Race in Dayton, Ohio on Memorial Day as my target 5k and then down shift to the 1,500 for the summer although I had no idea how to do that. I had run the Cox race a few years ago and it was almost as flat as the Brewery run. I really wanted to test myself more on the track but there seemed to be so few races on the oval for masters runners. Then one night as I was surfing the internet I stumbled upon masterstrack.com. I found a schedule for masters track events around the country and staring me square in the face was "USA Masters Outdoor Track and Field Championships, Eugene, Oregon, August 7-10." It also said that ANYONE (if you fit the age criteria) could participate. *Sonofagun, Pre, I have to get out there. This could be the culmination of my quest. This is where my journey has been taking me. It's been taking me to you.* Then I realized that August 6 was my anniversary. *Oh, shoot, Pre, this is going to be a tough sell.* I didn't mention this idea to anyone, and certainly not to my wife, for quite some time. Timing is everything. I couldn't fully explain my infatuation with Pre or Eugene. What was pulling me out there? Where do these ideas come from? What do they mean?

Of course, turning the Oregon idea into reality depended on a host of stars lining up, one of which was how my knee would respond to Pain and Torture and training. It had held up quite well from the Longaberger Mile, which I interpreted as a good omen. The possibility of running in Eugene energized me to dig in at PT. I attacked the work. Again, a reminder that you must have an idea of how you want to feel—I knew at some visceral level that running in Eugene would help me live my Dream—and you must make this feel big enough and powerful enough to get you through obstacles. Otherwise the obstacles will suck the energy right out of you, you won't perform as well, and you will recover less quickly from injury. In a way, the obstacles must become a part of the performance process. I was getting better at doing this, at embracing obstacles rather than getting mad at the world when something got in my way.

Embracing pain and torture is a lot easier when you get to run on an underwater treadmill (UWT). If we ever build a house, I'm going to have it designed to include one of these contraptions. My first time running on the underwater treadmill was an orgasmic-like experience. I was afraid to tell my wife that I was in love with a treadmill. How could something so hard on the body on land be so easy in the water? Because you're removing about 40% of your weight. I only weigh 90 pounds when running on the UWT and less impact forces equal no knee pain. The UWT treated me like a mother. It was forgiving of all of my funky leg structure and function. It loved me for what I was—it didn't care that my left leg was longer than the right or that I was bowlegged or that my natural gait was all screwed up. I was in a state of suspended euphoria.

No wonder the underwater treadmill is becoming more popular with athletes. Richard Seven writes in the *Seattle Times* that a variety of professional sports teams use the UWT for training. But it can also be used with people like me, who are rehabilitating an injury, or disabled people who need exercise. A study reported in *sportsinjurybulletin.com* examined the effects of the UWT on leg strength for patients who had undergone total hip replacement. Half of the 20 participants used the UWT for three weeks in addition to the standard protocol of physical therapy while the other half (control group) received just the standard protocol. The UWT individuals had significantly greater hip-abduction strength (strength while moving the leg laterally away from the body) compared with the individuals in the control group. This increased strength has been shown to assist hip replacement patients in developing the proper gait more quickly.

The downside to my UWT-induced euphoria was that running on the UWT combined with the dry land Pain and Torture activities Mark had me doing totaled about two hours each visit. I'm not sure if I could have justified this time without telling myself "Well, Jay, you do plan to write a book about these experiences." I have a much greater appreciation now for people, such as Stephen King, who commit to hundreds of hours of PT following a life-threatening accident or injury, just to get their life back to neutral. I was doing PT to get my athletic life back but it seemed somehow less important, which is part of the problem. As we get older, the malaise can begin to creep in. Robert McCammon captures this process in a passage in *Boy's Life*:

We all start out knowing magic. We are born with whirlwinds, forest fires, and comets inside us. We are born able to sing to birds and read the clouds, and see our destiny in grains of sand. But then we get the magic educated right out of our souls. We get it churched out, spanked out, washed out, and combed out. We get put on the straight and narrow and told to be responsible. Told to act our age. Told to grow up, for God's sake. And you know why we were told that? Because the people doing the telling were afraid of our wildness and youth, and because the magic we knew made them ashamed and sad of what they'd allowed to whither in themselves.

After you go so far away from it, though, you can't really get it back . . . Just seconds of knowing and remembering. When people get weepy at movies, it's because in that dark theater the golden pool of magic is touched, just briefly. Then they come out into the hard sun of logic and reason again and it dries up, and they're left feeling a little heartsad and not knowing why. . . .

The truth of life is that every year we get farther away from the essence that is born within us. We get shouldered with burdens, some of them good, some of them not so good. Things happen to us . . . Life itself does its best to take that memory of magic away from us. You don't know it's happening until one day you feel you've lost something but you're not sure what it is.

I cried the first time Doug shared that passage with me because I felt myself in it. I had become an academic (not that there's anything wrong with that). But competence does not equal passion or bliss. Just because I was fairly good at research and publishing it in academic journals didn't mean I had to or should do it for the rest of my life. I began to feel the malaise, that something wasn't quite right with the work I was doing. I got into sport and exercise psychology because I loved sport and exercise, not because I wanted to study it to death. But my graduate education had led me down the academic path, a path of theory, statistics, and dull-to-the-bone writing, pulling me further and further away from the magic, the magic of being an athlete, of playing with something physically, of challenging my whole being on a regular basis. Then, of course, kids came along, pets, loans, responsibilities, ambitious administrators, and benevolent oppressors (people who think they are helping you but are only helping themselves). And then as McCammon writes, *one day you feel you've lost something but you're not sure what it is.* All I can tell you is that you need to pay attention to these moments of self-awareness sooner rather than later. The athlete was calling me and I paid attention. I did something about it, which, of course, led me to my present predicament. Living your bliss doesn't mean that it's all fun and games. But at least you feel alive.

Similar to my first PT experience, I was once again enrolled in the patellar protection program. The general theory—and I call it a theory because no one in orthopedics or PT really knows what to do with people like me—proposes that weak upper leg strength and poor flexibility in people with a certain leg structure—which I have—are the main culprits of patello-femoral dysfunction, meaning that the patella tracks abnormally. I've gone over this before but think of it as optimal redundancy because I've found that most people don't hear all that well whenever they are told or read something for the first time. If your body type and certain mechanical conditions predispose you to a maltracking knee cap, you may not know it until you start doing dumb things such as running, which exposes the patellofemoral joint to a contact force seven times your body weight. And if you keep doing the same activity over and over and over and over and over and over and over and over (you get the idea), your out-of-whack patella starts mistreating your tendons.

The dry land protection program I was in had me doing leg presses, wall squats, retro lunges, a heel push motion on something called a fitter, terminal knee extension with a cable, multi-hip on a machine, and a strap walk to work the gluts (butt muscles). I'm sure you have come across these exercises before but based on my experiences over the past year and a half, you need to do three things as part of a patello-femoral protection program, especially if you have the body type and leg structure I have been describing:

1. Daily stretches (two times a day is better) focused on the hamstrings, hip flexors, quads, calves, and the gluts. The more elastic you can keep these muscles the less stress that is placed on the knee.

2. A regular, vigorous resistance training program (at least twice a week), such as the one I described previously. Running does not build muscle in the legs. In fact, as Costill's research showed us, runners who just run get weaker leg muscles as they get older. Plus, we lose muscle mass as we age. Strengthening the quads and gluts are especially relevant for us older athletes. Strong quads help to medially stabilize the patella and strong gluts help to prevent the upper leg from too much internal rotation when you run.

3. Use the principle of variability to prevent overuse injuries. Janet Dufek writes in the American College of Sports Medicine's *Health and Fitness Journal* that overuse injury is repetitive microtrauma to the neuro-musculo-skeletal (n-m-s) system. Importantly, most of us aren't aware overuse is occurring until it is too late and we're in the doctor's office begging for our referral to PT.

Before my latest bout with stupidity, I had vague ideas floating around in my head about the importance of varying the training routine. But the research on this hits me over the head: people who get injured don't vary the way they do things. Duh! Okay, let me say it another way: people who are injured least often perform more variably than people who are continually paying out money to their orthopedist and physical therapist. One study found that highly skilled runners who varied their foot strike (sometimes forefoot, sometimes midfoot) were less likely to be injured than runners who had the same foot contact pattern every time. A study out of Texas Tech examined the connection between injury proneness of jumpers and their biomechanical profiles when performing submaximal and maximal vertical jumps. The jumpers who performed with more variability during the submax jumps and the least variability in the max jumps had experienced the least number of injuries. The key to injury prevention is to vary your training pattern frequently within the same activity, what Dufek calls Within-Activity Cross-Training, the physiological outcomes of cross-training or variability training notwithstanding. The main point is that the variability principle gives masters athletes—especially us high risk ones—the best chance of avoiding injury and staying healthy so that we can train. The whole debate about the physiological pros and cons of different kinds of activities makes no sense to me. None of it matters if you can't train. You can't get better without consistent training. The overuse injuries occur at the submax level—the training level—when we keep doing the same things day after day after day.

If you love your primary activity and want to keep doing it then vary what you do. Dufek gives a variety of running suggestions for modifying and varying the pattern to avoid repetitive microtrauma:

- Incorporate hills
- Vary pace, distance, and time of run
- Carry light hand weights during the run
- Run on varied surfaces—track, trails, cinders, grass
- Reverse the direction of your running route
- Try deep-water running
- Run on a treadmill
- Rotate running shoes
- Take your dog with you
- And my own personal favorite—the underwater treadmill (The problem, of course, with this one is that you are already injured if using it.).

After coming to my senses and learning more about the importance of variability, I actually rode my new mountain bike that the family surprised me with on my birthday (last June) for the first time on a unseasonably warm, March day. After swiping away the cobwebs and pumping air into the tires I headed out on the country roads. It was gorgeous. I powered up the hills and whizzed down them. When I got back I rode around the neighborhood with my daughter on our bikes. My butt was sore the next day but it was worth it—the wait for spring was over.

21
LIVING ON THE SIDE OF THE MOUNTAIN

I had made it through the winter. The greatest challenge had been mustering up the motivation and energy to plow through PT and my training when I wasn't really sure what was on the other side. I found ways to enjoy the work and that is what got me through it, but there were those days . . . the days when your energy level is low, the benevolent oppressors are messing with you, and you're thinking, *Oh, forget it. Forget the training, forget the pain in the butt PT. Forget the retro lunges.* It is during these moments when you look up and see the peak of the mountain and begin to believe that getting to the summit is what being an athlete is all about.

Only it's not.

I think mountain climbers understand this better than most. Being an athlete is about living on the side of the mountain. That's where the experience of living, of feeling alive is found. Reinhold Messner, one of the top climbers in the world, writes, "To be out there in dangerous places, and trying to come back, was everything. I learned that the great moment is not reaching the summit; the coming back is the climax." And a great American climber, Yvon Chouinard, writes, "The purpose of risking your neck in an adventure is to attain some sort of spiritual and personal growth. This will not happen if you are so fixated on the goal that you compromise the process away."

So what is the process of becoming and sustaining the life of an athlete? If you've been following my so-called adventure, it's simple but not easy. You have lots of ideas, but if you're paying attention to your life, one of them hits you over the head repeatedly. This is your little voice of bliss—the feel that you like to have. Messner describes the beginning of this feeling alive process: "We climbers are dreamers. Before starting my expeditions, I always allow dreams to grow in my mind. If these dreams are strong, they grow into action." If you are true to yourself, you begin to prepare to experience your feel by engaging in the activity or activities—you take action—that are your best shot at experiencing it, which gives you a heightened sense of feeling alive. As you immerse yourself further into these activities, you face many dragons—some external, most internal—that must be slain. These inner demons are part of the process because as you get good, you want to get better; you set goals and begin to believe that reaching the summit is what being an athlete is all about. If you're not paying attention, you start thinking you have to work harder when you hit certain obstacles so that you can reach the summit. This is the sorcerer's evil trick because it seems appealing and logical but this way of living not only cannot be sustained but also limits enjoyment and improvement in the long run. The feel—your bliss—will die. You'll burnout, get frustrated, give up, or get into a training rut. And you won't get better. You'll stay on the performance plateau, not being able to go up and not able to come back. And remember what Campbell said, a hero is involved in a process of a going *and* returning, a coming back. You have to embrace obstacles as part of the process because they are ultimately what transform you. And that is what you bring back from your adventure of feeling alive. You can't make it back without obstacles. In fact, there is no adventure without them.

The Feeling Alive model (fig. 21.1) captures this holistic process for breathing life back into your life no matter your age. It's a metaphor for athlete.

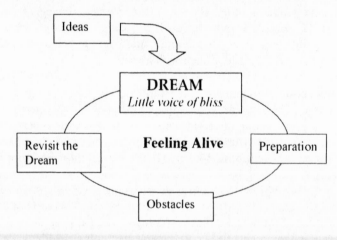

Figure 21.1 The Feeling Alive Model.

Doug had introduced this process for engaged living to me a number of years ago. I understood it intellectually but struggled to "live the model" or integrate the ideas into how I was living. In fact, I completed a version of the model (fig. 21.2) when I met with Doug a number of years ago during a spring break. On the upper left-hand side of the model, you can see that the Ideas for this project—becoming an athlete and writing about it—were already in my brain: Sporting, Thinking, Writing. Even more telling is the rough graph at the bottom of the page that documents my waning energy and self-expression at that time. I was kind of stuck in between preparation and obstacles and was not experiencing the deeper feel that was a part of me. I was losing myself or as I stated earlier in borrowing the line from Anne Tyler I was *turning into the wrong person*. I had without much conscious thought chosen a hollow achievement path instead of blazing my own trail of self-expression, which for me had for many, many years involved being an athlete. I needed to reconnect expression and achievement in my own way. This was my wakeup call.

Figure 21.2 The Feeling Alive Worksheet.

If you let life sidetrack you from this dynamic feeling alive process, you'll get stuck like the monkey in the South Indian Monkey Trap that Robert Pirsig describes in *Zen and the Art of Motorcycle Maintenance*. The trap, which is a coconut with rice inside, has a hole big enough for the monkey's hand to go in but not big enough for his fist to come out when he grabs the rice. No matter how hard the monkey works, he cannot get his hand out if he keeps holding on to the rice. You can't tell the monkey to "work harder" or "fight through the pain." The monkey is just stuck.

The same thing happens to us humans when we are tempted by the sum-mit sorcerer. When we begin to believe that achieving the goal—whatever tangible outcome we desire—is the main reason for partaking in the activity, we are trapped. Anyone who wants to become an athlete or live his or her Dream is going to face this trap sooner or later. I was in danger of succumb-ing to the trap while I waited for spring. I was beginning to view PT and some of my training as just an obstacle to my goal achievement. Racing, achieving, getting better times is what I wanted. I also noticed that my energy level and interest were waning. I'm sure it was partly the winter blahs but I was in danger of becoming the trapped monkey.

A few years ago I would have tried to work harder or I would have given up on myself or I would have just succumbed to the performance plateau. But this time I had a better understanding of what to do when you get to this point of being tempted by the summit sorcerer, but that's only because I paid attention to the feel I wanted in my life. I knew it was time to simply rediscover, rethink, slow down, reflect on why I had started the quest in the first place, what Doug calls *Revisit the Dream* and the final piece of the perfor-mance puzzle. I wanted to experience the feel of the lived athlete. That was my Dream. I wasn't doing physical therapy to get better; I was doing it to live my Dream of being an athlete. And it was part of the performance process, just as racing and training were. And I needed energy and motivation to perform and enjoy the Pain and Torture. Revisiting the Dream opens you back up and helps you reconnect with how you like to feel, which then re-energizes you so you can dig back in on things like preparation, training, and Pain and Torture. And the only constraints to Revisit are how closely you are paying attention and your creativity. I think I'm getting better at doing that.

I informed my wife that I was taking our five-month old puppy, Baxter, to the Miami track to do some intervals.

"Isn't there still snow on the track?" she asked.

"Yep," I replied. "But all I need to do is shovel one lane. And Baxter can run around because he'll be fenced in. "

"Okay," she said. I'm sure she was happy to get us both out of the house.

I didn't tell Kim that I needed to go Revisit my Dream but that was the main reason for going. I was learning that Revisiting is a vital part of sustain-ing life while living on the side of the mountain. As I started shoveling lane one, I couldn't help but think of my dad's line, "I never shovel snow as ordi-nary men do." And I recalled those times when as a young boy I would shovel the snow off of our driveway basketball court in sub-freezing temperatures so I could get the stuffing beaten out of me again by the cold and my brother. I was doing the same thing today except my shooting hoops was running some intervals and Baxter was playing the role of my brother. The shoveling was a workout in and of itself but I finally did get enough snow cleared to run some 200s (half a lap). I took a rest to stretch and to admire my work. Today wasn't about running anyway; it was really more about shoveling because the shoveling reminded me of the feel associated with being an athlete. I shoveled snow when I was younger because I wanted to play. I wanted to feel the ball in my hand, to see my breath, to hear the pounding of the ball, to swish one through the net. I wanted that feel so bad I was willing to shovel, shovel, and shovel some more in weather that was much colder than today.

I don't know if I'll ever experience quite the same feel now with running as I did when younger but I'm getting doggone close. I took off around the first turn, starting a little slow to test the footing. Baxter saw me go and decided to sprint with me or chase me. I'm not sure what was on his mind but being a puppy his coordination needed some work. Before I knew what hit me, Baxter had run into me and knocked me to the ground (Baxter is a 1/2 Great Pyrenees, 1/2 Golden Retriever so even though just a puppy, he has some smack to him.). I slid a few feet face down in the snow and as I rolled over Baxter jumped on me and licked my face. He seemed quite happy that he knocked over his master and I'm sure he wanted to play the running game again. My biggest fear was that I was injured so I did a quick body scan. Everything seemed intact so I walked back to the starting line to give it another shot, only this time I whipped out the slobbery tennis ball from one of my layers and threw it as far as I could. Baxter eagerly took off and so did I (in the opposite direction). There is nothing better than fast 200s, especially after shoveling. Baxter joined me at the finish, ball in mouth, ready to go again. We walked back to the start and I heaved the ball again. After about the fourth time, Baxter got tired and laid down at the start, waiting for me to finish up. I stopped after the sixth repeat, grabbed my shovel, and headed for home when I heard my mom call, "Jay, Greg, c'mon in. Time for dinner."

BELL LAP
TRANSFORMING TO MYSELF

"The hero must be true to himself, for then we know what he will do."
—David Norton

. . . A heaviness came over me on the backstretch unlike any I have ever known. I felt as if death was near. And then I was on the home stretch—the final 100 meters—and I felt lighter as if someone was carrying me along. But it was too late. I had lost too much time in the previous 200 meters. I imagined myself flying. I tried to catch the guy in front of me . . .

22
SHOCK THE SYSTEM

George Leonard, author of *Mastery*, describes a performance plateau as "the long stretch of diligent effort with no seeming progress." I want to explore a little more these ideas about the performance plateau and living on the side of the mountain since athletes, especially mature ones, spend so much time there. It seems to me that the key to living on the side of the mountain is to experience your Dream—a feel you like to have—while being an athlete. I would even suggest that this is the essence of the athlete. You're not moving up and you're not moving down. You're just doing your thing. When you do that, it makes the experience of the performance plateau an enjoyable one. Leonard writes:

> To love the plateau is to love the eternal now, to enjoy the inevitable spurts of progress and the fruits of accomplishment, then serenely to accept the new plateau that waits just beyond them. To love the plateau is to love what is most essential and enduring in your life.

This sounds good but to embrace the plateau you need to know for yourself *what is most essential and enduring in your life*. In my experience, most people either don't know what that is or if they do, they are afraid to live it out. For me, I kind of knew that being an athlete was an essential part of my life, the feel was missing, and I was afraid to go after it. I was afraid of what my colleagues might think, afraid that this work wouldn't be considered "scientific" and that I might never become a full professor, afraid that I wouldn't have time for my family, afraid that my best running performances were behind me, afraid that I would get injured. Geez, it's so easy to succumb to the fear of living what you feel. I don't why it's so hard to just be yourself, but it is. Parker Palmer writes about this in *Let your Life Speak*:

What a long time it can take to become the person one has always been! How often in the process we mask ourselves in faces that are not our own. How much dissolving and shaking of ego we must endure before we discover our deep identity—the true self within every human being that is the seed of authentic vocation.

I'm not exactly sure of the tipping point that catapulted me into the athlete journey to rediscover myself but I do know that that day at my son's soccer game the idea had become so strong that I just couldn't take it anymore. I just said, "Screw the fear." I had to turn the idea into a Dream that I could live or I would curl up and continue to be afraid of things that didn't matter all that much. I'm certainly not the only mature adult who has done this. People older than me have figured this stuff out for themselves. Sometimes it takes some time.

I read about Mavis Albin right about the time I had my re-awakening. At the age of 56, she had been invited to play three-on-three basketball in the Senior Olympics. "It changed my whole life," says Albin in an article about her in *Better Nutrition*. "The old competitive spirit returned." But what's more important is what led up to the invitation. "I absolutely loved basketball in high school," Albin says in a *USA Weekend* article. Then, like many women who matured in the 1950s, there was marriage and three sons to raise that put her love for basketball on hold for over three decades. "One day I read about the Senior Games in the paper, and I told my husband, 'I'd love to do that.' He said, 'Mavis, why don't you?'" She contacted the Louisiana Tigerettes 50+ team and, after a few workouts, they invited Mavis to join. She actually had to try out. I'm sure there was fear but because Mavis was paying attention to how she wanted to feel in her life, the desire grew until it overshadowed the fear, and enabled her to take action. "It's the most wonderful experience," Albin says about her senior basketball experiences. "It really helped me through a difficult period in my life. Being active, working out with people you like is great therapy." And Mavis got game. Her team has the won the gold a few times in the Senior Olympics. "I tell people they have no idea what they can accomplish until they get up and get down to business."

Sara Hall writes about her athlete-awakening story in *Drawn to the Rhythm: A Passionate Life Reclaimed*. Hall went from a physically inactive wife and mother to an age-group champion at the World Master Championships in the women's single shell (rowing). Only three years prior she was driving with her children along a harbor road when she spotted a tiny sliver of a boat, a single shell, making its way up the shoreline. The image was so powerful that Sara pulled the car over onto the shoulder to watch. She writes:

In the quiet thrust of the boat, the sweet swing of the sculler, I saw everything I wanted to be, everything I always had been beneath the sensible dresses and the sorrow. Found in that moment the mission of these hands, this body, this heart . . . Suddenly I felt engaged where I had been adrift, alert where I had been lulled by habit.

At that moment Sara knew that she had to start rowing. She had been driving on that road for years. Why that moment? Why that day? Because, like Mavis Albin, Sara Hall was paying attention to her life. *Drawn to the Rhythm* describes her experiences in becoming a masters athlete. Sara had it much tougher than me as she had to deal with some major personal and family issues. But the whole point is that she came back to life because sculling made her feel alive—and she knew it would. She found the desire, cultivated it, and then made it stronger than the fear. It's only when you engage in that process that you can have fun living on the side of the mountain because you will be living your Dream each and every day. Even days on the performance plateau will be better than days that you weren't an athlete.

Okay, so the plateau can be a fun thing if you know how you want to feel. But how do you get good? I've scientifically diagrammed my own performance plateau experience based on extensive research and meditation (fig. 22.1). The (P) is the label for Plateau, whereas the (B) is for Breakthrough. When I started my training to be a runner the plateaus were fairly short in duration, followed by a breakthrough of some kind, which usually resulted in faster race times. As I kept going, the plateaus got longer, either because of minor injuries or because that's just the way the performance process works. As I continue to chronologically age, I suspect the plateaus will begin to have a slight decline to them and be even longer. I wonder if you can have a decline Breakthrough? I hope so.

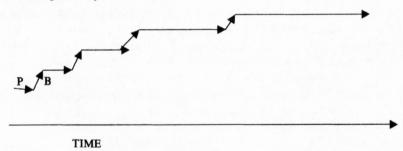

TIME

Figure 22.1 Plateau/Breakthrough Graph.

What you can take from this highly scientific graph—which I'm sure will be published in *Science* after my death—is that athletes, especially older athletes, spend most of their time on the plateau. When I look back at my performances over the past year and a half, my spring/summer 5K race times were about a 6:40 per mile pace. Then, I had some performance breakthroughs, such as at the Loveland and Brewery races, where my mile pace went from 6:40 to 6:30 to 6:10-6:20. That's a significant improvement. My times in the mile also improved relatively quickly. But now the plateaus were getting longer, which is why you have to enjoy living on the side of the mountain. Plateaus are a natural part of the performance process, but so are breakthroughs, if you are paying attention. What I found is that periodically I had to shock the system.

When I look back on my improvement in race times over the past year and a half, the breakthroughs were usually preceded by some kind of shock to the system. I don't know if this is a scientific term but I view it as a form of training that jars all of you—physical, mental, emotional, and spiritual. It takes you out of your comfort zone and moves you to another one. You need the shock to get you off of one plateau and on to the next one. I'm thinking this is how I got faster. When I reflect on my fall training, I can recall a number of shocks to the system but one in particular occurred just a few weeks before my Brewery breakthrough race.

I was standing in the parking lot of Hueston Woods State Park just outside of Oxford with the women in red cross-country team. We were there for what we all thought was the weekly long run at "moderate" pace. Coach Ceronie, who knows all about the shock theory, had other ideas. His plan for the day was to play Fartlek Poker. Fartlek is Swedish for "speed play" and the play consists of running on mixed terrain with varied paces. The idea is to add variety to a workout and prepare the body for the torture of racing—shock the system. Coach's version of Fartlek was to have a runner pick a card from several in his hand as he pedaled his bike along side us. The number on the card, which ranged from 1 to 5, would dictate how many minutes we would surge. Immediately another runner was to pick a card to tell us how many minutes we would run at recovery pace. And so on, and so on. We would do this for about 40 minutes after a 1-mile warm-up. My first thought was *this is nuts. I will die!* As we started out, Coach pedaled up to me and said, "Hey, Jay, just try to keep up with the back of the pack on the surges " (this, of course, meant that I had to run very fast). I still thought I was going to die as I was quite familiar with the 9-mile Hueston Woods loop. It should be called Hueston Hills, which is why I'm sure Coach chose it as the place to unveil his poker face.

The game began—2 minutes, 4 minutes, 1 minute (whew!), 4 minutes, and so on. We never knew what was coming next, which was a good thing. The lead runners would always come back to the pack as we recovered after each surge, which built on the idea that we were all in this together. I surprised myself by being able to run fast, even up the hills, and actually passed a few runners in the back of the pack on a couple of the surges. Then I heard Coach announce, "This is the last surge. When you're done just run a moderate pace for the mile and a half that you have left." And just like that it was over. Seven miles total. I was the last to reach the rendezvous point and got a high five from Andrea. The van arrived to take us back to where we had started the game. I had shocked the system. I had won and the award was a ride in the van where I could now appreciate the beauty of Hueston Woods, which is difficult to do when you are Fartleking. I smiled as I thought of the time I went out to Hueston Woods for my first planned, solo 7-mile run and then realized as I reached the 7-mile mark that there was no team van to pick me up and take me back to the start. I walked the remaining two miles to the car wondering if I was experiencing a boomer moment or just being an absent-minded professor.

There have been other shocks to the system throughout the quest, mostly involving my practice sessions with the women in red: 12 x 200 surges, 200 jogs on the track, 8 x 60 seconds as fast as I could go on the cinders, 10 x 400s and 7 x 800s on the x-country course. And each time I experienced a shock, I was thinking *this is the hardest workout I have ever done* (It's not a shock if you aren't thinking this). I don't do these kinds of workouts too often—certainly not as often as the younger women in red—as I am crazy but not stupid. You have to listen to your mind and body and know when you are ready for the shock. All I know is that for me the shocks are needed to get up to the next plateau, to live on the side of the mountain but moving a bit closer to the summit, a summit that may never be reached. The shocks remind you to enjoy the plateau but don't get too comfortable with it. I would say this is one of the major differences between masters athletes and mature adults who exercise—athletes shock the system through periodic bouts of hard training and racing to avoid getting trapped in the performance rut.

23
THE JOY OF DELIBERATE PRACTICE

Certainly shocks to the system timed right help you get good. But still, you can't build your athletic life on them because they're too infrequent. Getting good as an athlete demands that you commit to the everyday training, which will only happen if you pay attention to how you want to feel. This engaged training builds your foundation so that you're ready for the shocks. Some performance scientists call this "deliberate practice."

Before we dig in on the deliberate practice process for how athletes get better, you should be forewarned that an analysis by an economist (yes, an economist) in *Journal of Sports Sciences* showed that the top running performances by American men and women come between the ages of 27 to 30. After age 30, a gradual decline is seen in average running speed for endurance events—5k and up. But the analysis also reveals that the rate of slowing down for runners 30 and older is "amazingly low for both men and women" until we reach age 70. And as I stated earlier many of us were not fully engaged in consistent, deliberate practice when younger. I point this out for the results-oriented reader who may be delaying getting into the athlete mode because you are asking, "What's the point, I'm past my prime?" The point is that you can become a pretty darn good endurance-based athlete—or anything really—in middle age and beyond. The fact that you are chronologically older is of little consequence. Of course, if you are thinking this way you are kind of missing the whole point of the become-an-athlete story. The real point to engaging in the athlete part of your life is to feel alive.

The relevance for us mature folks is that, yes, our physical performances decline as we age but the scientific literature suggests that well-trained masters athletes are able to maintain relatively high levels of performance once the physical peak has been passed. And the way they do that is through deliberate practice. My main interest in this adventure has been to explore the reason WHY I would want to partake in deliberate practice in the first place. In the long run, that's the more important issue than how I should train because I won't do the how consistently unless I am clear on the why. Now that I've reached a point of inner clarity on the why, the deliberate practice concept seems more relevant and interesting.

K. Anders Ericsson, a psychologist at the University of Florida, suggests that engagement in deliberate practice requires effort, generates no immediate rewards, and is motivated by the goal of improving performance rather than inherent enjoyment. I'm not sure I agree completely with his definition—especially the lack of enjoyment part—but deliberate practice is needed when part of your intent is to get better at some activity. No surprise in that Ericsson and his colleagues' research has found that the performers who get really good spend a lot more time than their less-than-stellar performers—practicing!

Masters runner Ed Whitlock just may be the world's greatest deliberate practicer. Each morning he jogs around the Evergreen Cemetery, located two blocks from his house in Milton, Ontario (Canada)—for two to three hours! Ed, whose story has been highlighted in as many magazines as Hugh Hefner, is the Forrest Gump of his generation. He just runs the same loop over and over again. Alone. "I find it a drag," he said, when interviewed by Michael McGowan for www.saturdaynight.ca. "It's just something that has to be done." The reason it has to be done is that the deliberate practice keeps Ed on his game. A few years ago, Ed became the first septuagenarian (70 plus) to break the three-hour barrier for a marathon. And before that he ran the Columbus Marathon in 2:52:50, which set a record in the 69 year-old category. Ed intuitively understands a major deliberate practice principle: he continues to increase his workload. "I don't think you ever really stop the slide," he says. "You can't do that. If you train the same way you did last year, all things being equal, you're going to run a slower time. The only way you can hold your own is by doing more training."

But it's not just the quantity of training that gets you better or prevents the age-related performance slide from turning into an avalanche. Ericsson points out that humans tend to be attracted to automaticity, meaning that after we attain a certain level of performance we shift into an autopilot phase that takes the least amount of mental and physical effort. Performers who get stuck in this stage only maintain a certain level of performance—they don't get better or as they get older experience dramatic performance declines—that Ericsson calls arrested development. Ericsson writes, "The expert performer actively counteracts such tendencies towards automaticity by deliberately constructing and seeking out training situations in which the set goal exceeds their current level of performance." And this principle applies whether you are a musician, a teacher, a parent, or a runner. Shock the system, baby! You have to make yourself vulnerable in new training and performance situations in order to get better. And to do that you must work on your desire becoming stronger than the fear. That's why you need to spend a lot of time on the front end of your life thinking about and reflecting on *how you want to feel in moments of action.*

Pure deliberate practice is not all fun and games. It can't be. Deliberate practice is a conscious attempt to make something painful—physically, mentally, and emotionally. You will fail at first as you engage in the process of developing a whole new set of physical, cognitive, and emotional skills needed to take you to the next level. But this failure is essential to improvement because it forces you to search for ways and means to develop more skilled and refined action. It forces you to pay attention to the details, to the minutiae of performance. The experts don't just keep practicing what they have already learned over and over again. They avoid the drudgery of routine. One study found that elite-level figure skaters fell more in practice than sub-elite skaters because they were practicing more jumps they hadn't already mastered.

And older is better or at least not worse. A study by Ericsson found that 60-year-old expert pianists, who continued to give public solo performances, maintained speeded performance on piano-related tasks that compared favorably with much younger expert pianists. And the older expert pianists were able to maintain this high-level performance on about 10 hours per week of deliberate practice, much less than their younger counterparts. So once you get good, you can still perform at a fairly high level with less practice, as long as the practice you perform is deliberate, meaning that you devote full attention and concentration to whatever it is you are practicing.

I'm not sure if this is the perfect example of older being better, but Phyllis Shipman comes to mind. Phyllis was highlighted in a *USA TODAY* article (March 11, 2003) as one of the best female archers in the United States. We're not talking about the masters or senior level of competition—Phyllis competed at the Olympic Trials in June 2004 but did not make the team. Her story follows a similar pattern for mature women in that she was introduced to archery as a young girl, participated as a collegian, and then forgot about it for years as she worked as a special educator and principal and raised a family. Phyllis's story epitomizes the feeling alive, becoming an athlete, and getting good at any age process. In 1996, Phyllis stumbled across an archery shop while on a business trip with her husband, which brought back sweet memories. She bought some equipment and started shooting in her backyard. She says, "I became so mentally refreshed in an hour of shooting. It was addictive and very seductive. The mental energy drew me into the sport." Recall Marie-Louise's comment about the energy of the race drawing her back? Then Phyllis joined an archery club, retired in 1998, and got interested in getting good. She was the oldest full-time resident athlete at the U.S. Olympic Training Center's Easton Sports Archery Complex in Chula Vista, California when she was preparing for the Trials. Interviewed for a story in *AARP The Magazine* about older being better, Phyllis says, "I'm at a point where I've made a lot of life decisions. I've raised a family. I'm not clouded by what the future will bring. That helps my focus." As you can see, the transformation to athlete took awhile but Phyllis is engaged in the entire experience. She says, "Retirement is your moment of freedom to follow your dream . . . At first I felt silly saying 'I'm an archer.' Now I don't bat an eyelash. Some days I think I'm like a snake who's shedding its skin . . . It's a metamorphosis."

We don't have to wait for retirement to begin this process of living our Dream, of committing to deliberate practice, nor should we. I will never be a world-class pianist, but I can feel alive and use the principle of deliberate practice to get good—whatever that ends up being for me—right now. What I'm learning is that the really good ones pay attention to little things and do things differently from the masses. Michael Jordan and Tiger Woods come to mind, and so does Ed Whitlock. What do these young and old great athletes pay attention to? The small stuff that on a day-to-day basis adds up to produce dramatically different results and prepares the mind and body to optimally respond to shocks to the system that lead to breakthroughs. The author of *Don't Sweat the Small Stuff* could not have been an athlete. I know the intent of the book was to help people be less stressed and not worry so much about small, unimportant things in our lives. But when you are fully engaged, when you are feeling alive, when you want to get good, details matter. And focusing on the details is not stressful. It's just a part of the performance process that you commit to because you love what you do.

Dan Chambliss, a sociology professor at Hamilton College, calls this process the *mundanity of excellence*. Many years ago he studied the nature of excellence in swimmers of all abilities by living with them, and interviewing them. The ones who won Olympic gold or who reached international status continually performed a series of actions, small skills, and activities that fitted together into a synthesized whole. Chambliss concluded: "The simple doing of certain small tasks can generate huge results. Excellence is mundane."

Joe Torre, former manager of the New York Yankees, talked about his all-star shortstop Derek Jeter for years as an athlete who made many big plays throughout his career. Torre has said that Jeter reflects the Yankee philosophy: think small, play big. Think small, PLAY BIG! That's what athletes who get good do, that's what anyone who gets good at anything does. One late night I was watching the Bob Costas show *On the Record* and he was interviewing comedian Jerry Seinfeld, the king of quirky observations. Costas asked Seinfeld how he got so good. "I like taking something, anything and making it excellent," Seinfeld replied. Costas followed up with something like, "But how do you see things and make them funny?" Seinfeld said, "I see and work on the details of things that most people miss." Top performers think small and PLAY BIG, and I doubt very much if they use a lot of goal setting, mental imagery, and confidence training, the staples of traditional sport psychology. It is the athletes who do the small things better than the rest of us, who combine the mundane with their "natural" ability, that leads to superlative performances maintained over many years. Hard work is overrated by coaches and the media. Lots of people work hard. The ones who get good work differently.

William Blake, the English visionary and artist, referred to the mundanity of excellence in his *Jerusalem* poem, "Labour well the Minute Particulars: attend to the Little Ones . . . He who would do good to another must do it in Minute Particulars." So this works not only for yourself but also when you might be helping others get good. And what seems interesting to me is that the process I've been using to become an athlete parallels the mundanity of excellence process for getting good. You are not going to pay attention to minute particulars or put in the deliberate practice time unless you are fully engaged in the moment of action. And, again, how do you get fully engaged? You know how you want to feel, you prepare for that feel, you embrace obstacles, you revisit the feel again and again. In his study of the best swimmers, Chambliss discovered that "they found challenges in small things: working on a better start this week, polishing up their backstroke technique next week, focusing on better sleep habits, planning how to pace their swim."

The deliberate practice needed for getting good doesn't have to be done solo but Ericsson's research suggests that the best violinists, for example, spent more time in solitary practice than violinists who didn't get as good. He writes, "When the experts practiced by themselves, they focused with full concentration on improving specific aspects of their music performance. . . ." Ericsson's studies find a consistent and strong relationship—especially in activities that are performed solo, such as music, darts, individual sports—between solitary deliberate practice and quality of performances. This doesn't mean that to get good you have to turn into an athletic hermit, but deliberate practice on your own seems important. This makes me feel a little better since, as I mentioned earlier, much of my become-an-athlete time has been practicing and training by myself. Solitude can be good. One of my former mentors at Purdue, Bill Harper, writes about the glory of being alone in sport:

Man must realize that he is before he can attempt an understanding of who he is. And it is in this state of aloneness, a state of solitary presence within-one's-self, that one may realize his uniqueness . . . Being alone is, in a sense, a oneness; a singularity; a unity within one's self. And being aware of this whole or total state one can truly understand that he is . . . In the aloneness of sport man is potentially able to realize that he is—that he is unique—that there is no other person like him in the world.

Throughout this feeling alive quest I have been discovering things about myself that usually occur when no one else is around. When I'm alone in my sacred place, I realize that I still have it in me to commit to deliberate practice. That pleasure can be found in the pain. That I am still free to explore who I am and what I want. That I can still experience the magical combination of rhythm, power, and speed. That when I experience these, I am expressing myself. That I can break rules. That I am free to decide how to live my life and muster up the courage to do it. That it is my responsibility to be the athlete and the person I want to be. A lot of good happens when you're alone. Becoming an athlete again has helped me see that more clearly. When you are alone, fully immersed in the mundanity of excellence and paying attention to the minute particulars, you are transcended. Gregory Jones, writing in *Christian Century* about mundane excellence with one's faith, uses a quote from Kathleen Norris, author of *The Quotidian Mysteries*: "It is a paradox of human life that in worship, as in human love, it is in the routine and the everyday that we find the possibilities for the greatest transformation." Amen.

24

A Funny Thing Happened on the Way to, During, and After the Race

Racing, testing, competing is the culmination of the athlete experience. Once you get hooked on racing, you can't go back to just exercising because every race heightens the experience of feeling alive; every race has hidden potential for transcendence and transformation. You would think that as you get good that racing would be more fun. Not true. It's all relative. The race, the competition always pushes you out of your comfort zone, whatever it might be at that moment. But no matter what happens, each and every race has its "aha!" moment—that moment of heightened awareness, of greater understanding about yourself or others, or just questions about the world around you. Sometimes these moments occur before, sometimes during, and sometimes after the race. I race to test myself but I also do it to experience these moments that make me feel alive. Just pay attention and you'll see that every race, every competition has an "aha!" just for you.

February 9—5K race, Middletown, Ohio. This was my first race following the Longaberger Mile and I was using it as a testing ground for my knee. My pace the first two miles was between 6:00 and 6:10. I was feeling good. Then I hit the infamous third mile and I could feel the slow down bug hit. My goal usually in the third mile is to not let anyone pass me, especially in a small-town race where the numbers are less, which increases my chances of achieving the goal. One woman passed me, then, a few seconds later, two more. *What the heck is going on? Where are these women coming from?* I swear I felt one woman elbow me as she went by. These women were waxing me and there was nothing I could do about it. I tried to fight back but there was nothing in the tank. As they pulled away, I had mixed feelings. Part of me felt like a male, sexist pig. Why was I so mad that these women were passing me? Where was that coming from? In many of the small-town races that I run in I compete with the first-place woman. The crowd always cheers for this woman. Why? Because women are still the underdog in sports and people like to see women compete with and hold their own against men. When I hear the cheers for the woman runner, my pig-headed maleness erupts and I get this stupid feeling that it is my birthright to uphold male dominance. As I helplessly watched the three women head to the finish, I felt that I had let the guys down. I was beaten by not one, not two, but three women. *What a wimp, I am.* The other part of me was ecstatic. With a daughter who loves to play sports such as soccer and running, these women were blazing a trail for Carly. Almost anything will be possible for Carly in sports. This wasn't always the case. It's only been 20 plus years since the women's marathon has been an Olympic event. Women and running is a relatively recent phenomenon. Fifty years ago, Marie-Louise couldn't run the mile race with the boys at camp and then she broke records. I never know what to experience when a woman passes me near the end of a race—sexist-pig anger or you-go-girl adulation. The fact that I even have this two-faced way of thinking makes me cringe.

February 23—2-mile race at Northern Kentucky University, Highland Heights, Kentucky. This is primarily a couples race with a Valentine's Day theme but since shorter distance races are so rare, and with vague visions of running the 1,500 in Eugene in August, I wanted to give it a shot. I tried to get my family to come with me to keep the V-Day theme alive. The night before I had them leaning towards coming with me but I should have known better. My experience in trying to rouse them at dawn further ingrained in my brain that, for me, the racing experience was a solo affair.

"C'mon Kim, wake up, it's time to go to my race," I said more loudly then normal. "We'll stop on the way and get you your favorite—a Grande Decaf Mocha, skim milk, no whip cream, extra foam (After years of failure, I had finally automated this phrase to appease my wife's exasperated, "How many times do I have to tell you!").

"Coffee is old news," Kim said, rolling over to my side of the bed. Strike one!

I headed to Carly's room where after a few minutes of searching, I was able to uncover her under an avalanche of blankets.

"Carly, honey, remember the race," I said in my firm but gentle Dad's voice. "Did you want to come with me? It's only 2-miles. We can be partners and maybe win a prize."

"I'm a miler," I heard a voice say from somewhere underneath the snow-covered hills. As I walked out of her room I heard the roar of the blankets rolling back over her. Strike two!

Entering my son's room I was proud to see that even though it was dead of winter, Colin had only his sheet over him. That's my boy! Surely he'll want to come with his Dad to the big race.

"Colin, Colin, remember the race. You said you wanted to come with me. This race has some great bagels and snacks to eat afterwards." I was giving it my best shot as Colin eats each meal like it is his Last Supper.

"Where is the race?" Colin said as he looked at me with slits for eyes.

"It's in Northern Kentucky, just over the river from Ohio. It won't take too long to get there." I didn't tell him that it was about an hour's drive as Colin takes after Grandpa Kimiecik who thinks that any trip of more than a few miles requires a passport and visa.

"Kentucky? That's out of state," he said as he grabbed his doggie and blanky and went back to dreaming about hitting Ken Griffeyesque home runs.

Strike Three! The Mighty Ageless Athlete had struck out. Alone, I ran a 5:50 first mile and 6:20 second mile and afterwards thought of Colin as I reveled in the food and watched the other happy couples.

April 12—1,500 meter race at Miami University Invitational, Oxford, Ohio. Coach Ceronie had talked me into running my first-ever outdoor 1,500.

"It will be a good test to see where you're at," he said.

"But I'll get killed by these college studs. I'll look like a fool." (It was déjà vu all over again). "Can I run with the women?" I asked half-kiddingly.

"No, Jay, you can't run with the women."

"But, why not? My times are more competitive with the women than with the men. Can't you use my age as a handicap or something?" Will I get lapped again?"

"This is outdoors, Jay, the track is bigger. If you run about 5:00, you won't get lapped, even by the guys."

I had been learning that some college meets are invitationals, where anyone can sign up and compete with the college athletes. No other college sport that I can think of does this as part of its business as usual. Can you imagine the Miami football team allowing me to play quarterback for a series of downs? Or how about the basketball team giving me a few minutes at point guard? It just wouldn't happen. Track and field can get away with the invitational because it's an individual rather than an interactive sport (except for the relays). And, in fact, many invitationals attract graduated, unattached athletes who are as good if not better than the college participants. This wasn't my case, obviously, as my first thought was that I'd rather run with the women than the men.

I lined up for the "slow" heat of the men's 1500. The gun went off and there I was—alone again as the 13 college studs took off like greyhounds after the electric bunny. Once again I was in a race against myself. My goal was 5:00, which works out to be about 80 seconds per lap for three laps and a 60 second 3/4 lap to finish it off. I got to work. It was very hard not to try to stay with the pack but I knew that would be suicidal. Even still, my first lap was 72. *Yikes! Slow down.* On the second lap my arms felt as if they were going to fall off. *No one told me about this feeling.* But I made it in 81 so I had seven seconds to spare. As expected, the third lap was a killer. I love the third lap because it's where everything in life happens. Face it: the first lap of any project is easy. Everything is new and fresh. You're like a kid in a video game store. You've got lots of ideas, lots of good feelings, lots of possibilities. The second lap you need a bit more focus; you start to prepare, you do a little work, but still not too bad. The third lap is where character is tested. The project can begin to get hard; you can begin to lose sight of why you started in the first place. You can get bogged down in the dark side, seeing all of the reasons why you shouldn't continue. This is where the little voice of bliss has to pull you through. *I hear cheering. Wow. The crowd is cheering my name. "Go, Dr. Jay. Go, Dr. Jay" Okay, that is way cool. Keep it together. Embrace the pain. Express yourself.* As I came around the turn to begin my final 300 meters, I heard Coach Ceronie yell, "You're right at four minutes. Get going. Pump those arms." *No way. I couldn't have slowed down that much.* I was mad (I found out later from one of the Miami women runners that I was actually at 3:57, an 84-second third lap). I think Coach was trying to create the urgency. Good move, Coach, because somehow the anger helped me refocus. I Revisited. I dug up the gas I had left. I was able to hold on and finish in 4:57 with a 60-second final 300 meters.

After the race, I rewarded myself with a cheeseburger and hot-dog from the concession stand outside the track. While eating, I did some quick calculations: I would need to cut off about 12 seconds or so to make it out of the qualifying race in my age group and into the finals at the Master Outdoor Track and Field Championships.

May 16—Rat Race 5k, Loveland, Ohio via Los Angeles, California. This was a Friday evening race and was on the same course where I had first experienced that breakthrough feel of an athlete back in September. This would be a good comparison test. As I sat in a traffic jam that combined rush hour traffic with other rats trying to get to the race, it dawned on me that the race title was very appropriate. It's difficult to avoid the rat race, where you end up doing a lot of the same things that everyone is doing, and wondering why you are doing them. I blasted the music to try to distract myself from thoughts that I was going to be late for the race.

To pass the time, I reminisced to a time over 20 years ago when I decided to run my first road race after moving to Los Angeles—the world's greatest rat race. I was living with a UCLA undergraduate student and his "I'll just stay the night again" girl friend in a one-bedroom, squalorous apartment on Purdue Avenue just off of Santa Monica Boulevard in West LA. I was posing as a graduate student in sport psychology at UCLA but had no real idea what I was doing with my life. At the time, running and my love for Kim were about the only things that made sense to me. I chose the "Festival of Lights" race to be held on a Sunday morning at Balboa Park, which was up in the valley in Encino.

My friend, Gary, a valley native, informed me that "Balboa is beautiful, for sure."

"Can you get there by bus?" I asked as I was one of the downtrodden in LA without a car.

"You can get anywhere in LA by bus, man. Call the RTD."

After hanging up from a conversation with a Rapid Transit Division employee, I realized that getting to the race would be far more difficult than running in it. I would need to rise at 5:00 a.m. on race day to take the first of three buses to get me to Balboa in time for the race. I would cruise through West LA, Beverly Hills, West Hollywood, and then up to the Valley, in about a two-hour journey. It was foolish. But don't we all have some stories in our foolish archives?

As bus #1 rumbled into West Hollywood (nearing my first transfer point), I was amazed at how many people were actually on the bus at this hour. At one stop, I noticed three weird looking characters walk on (remember, I'm in LA), but the most bizarre was a fellow (I think it was a fellow) dressed only in a tutu. *Don't sit next to me, please don't sit next to me.* Of course, he sat next to me and he wanted to flirt.

"Where ya going, guy?"

"I'm headed up to the valley to run a race."

"Hey, cool," he said. "I wish I had the energy to run, but I need to get my life together first."

"Don't we all," I replied, nodding that I understood his dilemma. "Well, here's my stop. Gotta go."

My newfound friend gave me a thumbs up sign as the bus rumbled away. I looked at my watch, which indicated I had only a 15-minute wait to catch bus #2 that would get me to the valley. I waited in the dark of LA. Fifteen minutes. Thirty minutes. Forty five minutes. No bus. *Where is the bus? I'm screwed!* I sat down on the bench to ponder my next move. A cart lady was walking towards me. *Oh, man. This is all I need.*

"Hey, mister," a weak voice called out. "You got any change to spare."

I reached into my bag, pulled out a quarter, and placed it in her shaking palm.

"Thanks, mister.

"You're welcome."

She just stood there, staring at me for a few seconds, which made me a bit nervous. *Runner killed by cart lady at Hollywood bus stop. Not sure what he was doing there.*

Finally. "Where ya going, mister?"

"I'm going up to the valley to run a race. How 'bout you?"

"I got nowhere to go," she said. "This here cart's my home. But I got a schedule to keep. It's 6:00 a.m. and I got to find me some breakfast."

I nodded . . . *How could such a seemingly together person be homeless?*

"Wait a second. What time did you say it was?"

"Six o'clock. I found this nice watch, and . . . "

"But isn't it seven o'clock?"

"Where ya been, mister, time change last night. Fall back, remember?"

Holy smokes. The time change. I forgot to set my clock back.

"But how did you . . . never mind." I reached into my bag. "Here. Here's five dollars," I said as I stuffed the money in her hand. "Go get yourself a good breakfast."

"Thanks, Mister."

As the cart lady walked away my bus pulled up—right on time. As it headed to the valley, I looked back and saw the cart lady shaking her head. I'm sure she got a good laugh out of that one.

I laughed as well. I had actually woke up at 4:00 a.m. to get to a 10k race on time.

The bus driver told me that Balboa Park was only a couple of miles from the drop off point. I jogged the rest of the way, rather than wait for bus #3. When I saw runners with race numbers on the front of their shirts, I knew I had made it. I ran well, finishing in 42:40, which at the time was a personal best. Running in the race was the easy part. I could make a long story even longer but I won't. I'll save the story for how I got home for another traffic jam.

Back to the rat race. My experience over the years, especially the last year and a half when I've picked it up a notch or two athletically, is that running in the race or participating in your sport of choice is the easy part. We're all natural athletes. I don't believe anyone who says, "I'm not very athletic." Not true. Your body is good at something and wants to be pushed, tested, and challenged on a regular basis. It wants to be an athlete. But it's easier to get caught up in the daily grind, the rat race, as we get older. There's just more crap to deal with, most of it of our own making. A big part of being an age-less athlete or peak performer is to protect what is easy. When I do intervals on the track. That's easy. When I run on the trails. Easy. When I pound out my weights. Easy. Getting to the track, getting to the trails, getting to the Rec Center. That's hard because the rat race gets in the way. Things that are unimportant and urgent can easily cloak over your bliss or the feel you like to have as an athlete, which are lurking just below the surface of your experiences. You must protect what is easy and I don't mean by building walls around the easy. You protect what is easy by living it, by experiencing it, by feeling it. The bigger you make the Dream—the feel you like to have—the easier it is to make decisions about when and where to experience your blissful energy at any given moment.

I was a few miles and minutes from the start of the Rat Race and the traffic was still bumper-to-bumper. I pulled into a restaurant lot and jogged to the registration area—just as I did years ago. Thinking about my younger years—when you go off on an adventure and don't even think about how to get back—had energized me. No one passed me in the third mile, I beat the first-place woman by a few seconds (despite a large crowd of females cheering her on), and my time was 23 seconds faster than my September race. As John Mellencamp sings, "Some days you're golden."

May 26—16th Annual Lou Cox Memorial 5K, Dayton, Ohio. This would be end of the road for me, literally, as Coach Ceronie had told me that if I was serious about the 1,500 in Eugene I should cut back on 5k road races. I hadn't officially decided about going to Oregon in early August but my little voice—which had grown quite large—was pulling me out there. The day before the race, I was the invited speaker at the Pre-Race Expo. I spoke to a small crowd and as part of the fun and had them predict my time in tomorrow's race. I would send a free copy of my *Intrinsic Exerciser* book to the person whose guess was closest to my actual time. I told them my time in last year's race was 20:50 but that I had been training hard this past year.

Two older gentlemen came up to me afterwards and introduced themselves as Harry and Larry. Larry was blind. Together they told me of how Larry runs in races using Harry as his guide. I always enjoy these kinds of conversations that come out of nowhere.

"We'll be out there tomorrow," Larry said.

"I'll be looking for ya, Larry," I replied. He reached out his hand and I shook it firmly. It's easy to be a hero when you surround yourself with people like Larry.

Before the race, I checked out the bulletin board that was covered with articles about Lou Cox, a running fanatic and fitness guru, who worked for the YMCA in Dayton for many years. He passed away in 1987 and this race began as a tribute to his dedication in bringing the fitness message to folks in the Miami Valley. Just before the race, a young woman sang the National Anthem so well that I started crying. *Keep it together, Jay.* The gun sounded and a thousand of us Coxians took off on the flat out and back course along the Great Miami River that ended on the track inside the University of Dayton's Welcome Stadium. The six-minute first mile seemed tolerable. I turned around and as I neared the second-mile mark, I saw them—Harry and Larry. Harry was holding Larry by the arm and they were running in perfect cadence. "Go Harry and Larry," I shouted as I passed. The second-mile electronic board split read 12:15. The race was on. Now it was time to slay the dragon that was the third lap. I felt a surge of power well up from somewhere. I crossed back over the river and headed for the Welcome track, headed for my sacred place. The Dream was carrying me along now. The paying attention, the mundanity of excellence had paid off. I waxed people right and left in the final 300 meters. A sub 19:00 seemed possible but I missed it by 11 seconds. Still, 19:11, almost two minutes faster than last year. *Screw the rat race, I'm going to Oregon.*

Dear Ray,

You are the lucky winner of The Intrinsic Exerciser since you predicted my time in the Lou Cox Memorial Race would be 19:02. Great guess work. You had me faster by only nine seconds. I appreciate your optimism. Enjoy the book. Good luck in your future races.

Take Care,

Jay

I can't remember the entire story but Ray had almost died, I believe, from a heart attack and was quite a prolific local runner before that. He didn't run this year's race. His silvery hair and slight build led me to estimate his age in the 70s. He probably knew better than the others what deliberate practice could do for an athlete.

Thank you, Harry and Larry and Ray, and most of all, thank you, Lou Cox.

25
WANTED DEAD OR ALIVE

As I approach middle age I've been thinking more about death, not so much in a fearful way but more out of curiosity. How will it happen? When will it happen? I could have died a number of times already, like the time I took a friend home from a college party, fell asleep at the wheel, and ended up in the woods. Or when I got this viral infection of unknown origin around the time Carly was born. It lasted for months and culminated by me fainting at her christening. I really thought I was going to die. Back then I was just trying to survive. These days I think a bit more seriously about how—and if—I will be remembered. How can I live my life today so that my family, my friends, and people I never met can take something from my life whether I'm dead or alive? I keep going back to Campbell's suggestion that "Any world is a valid world if it's alive. The thing to do is to bring life to it, and the only way to do that is to find in your own case where the life is and become alive yourself."

Exploring the life of the athlete has woken me up. I feel alive when I'm training or racing. This is when I am fully human, when I am expressing who I am and what I want. At the moment, running around an oval track seems to draw out my optimal self-expression. Thirty years ago it was soccer or basketball or baseball. Twenty years ago it was golf and tennis. Who knows what it might be five years from now, ten years from now. The track is what brought me back to life right now and I'm running with it. I feel authentic because I'm living my Dream on a regular basis, which has begun the transformation of me back to myself if that makes any sense. By bringing life back to me, I can only hope I'm wanted dead or alive. If you're paying attention to your life, being authentic, expressing who you are, you can inspire people whether you are dead or alive. Lou Cox can attest to that.

My first close-to-home experience with death was in the early 1970s when I was a teenager. I was in my bedroom playing Strat-o-Matic Baseball, the greatest sports board game ever invented. I think the Reds were playing the

Mets and I was right in the middle of making a crucial decision about whether to pull Tom Seaver for a relief pitcher when there was a knock on the door.

"I'm busy," I said.

"It's your mother."

"Oh . . . uh, what is it, mom?"

"Can I come in?"

"Sure."

So my mom comes in and as I look up I can see that she is distraught and has been crying.

"Grandpa Charlie had a heart attack and passed away."

"You mean he's dead."

"Yes."

And then mom left and closed the door behind her.

I can remember sitting there for a few seconds, not knowing quite how to respond. I felt that I should cry as Grandpa Charlie (my mom's father) was a good man. He killed a big black snake in our front lawn once. But tears wouldn't come. So I pulled Tom Seaver and rolled the die. I got back to living. I wasn't much interested in death and dying back then. I was interested in playing my game. I remember feeling a little guilty but that didn't stop me from getting back to the game.

I didn't know it then but I do now—death is all around us. But that can't stop you from playing the game. I cry easily now when death hits home. The main thing I get from it is that life as we know it is gone in the blink of an eye, the snap of a finger. I feel a connection with some people who have died because they were out there living the life of the athlete, getting closer to real freedom—knowing who they were and how to express that.

In late June I was in Portland, Maine presenting at the University of Southern Maine's Sport Psychology Institute—I love speaking at this event as the annual sojourn allows me to run along Casco Bay. I was eating breakfast in my hotel room, reading the local paper, when I stumbled upon the obituaries. Kyle Fitzherbert had just passed away. I noticed that Kyle died on June 26—the day I was born. He was only 14, the age at which I was introduced to death. When he was one, Kyle was diagnosed with Niemman-Pick Disease, an extremely rare disorder that stunts growth and caused him to depend on an oxygen tank for the last eight years of his life. Doctors predicted he would not make it to age 2. He certainly fooled them. Kyle had a special passion for music and baseball. He was a member of three bands and when he played the drums you could only see the drumsticks moving through the air. Kyle couldn't play baseball so he helped his dad coach Little League and also helped out with the local high school baseball team. His father said about Kyle, "He was really a gift to his community."

In July, I was on vacation with the family visiting my parents in New York. We had just arrived after spending a week in New Hampshire. It was getting closer to my trip to Oregon to participate in the Masters Championships and the fear was beginning to rear its ugly head. I picked up a stack of the local papers that had been left unread while we were up North. My eye caught a headline, "Advertiser sales representative dies in bike collision with farm tractor." Sharon Giannino, a 41-year old mother of three, loved cycling and was just finishing up a Saturday morning, 34-mile bike ride around Florida's onion fields with other area cyclists. As I read on, the description of her death (I later got more details from my dad) turned into something out of the Twilight Zone. As Sharon was pedaling furiously to reach the finish line, she had her head down to help her pedal faster and make her more streamlined. This caused her bike to drift into the path of an oncoming farmer's tractor that was puttering towards her on Round Hill Road. Sharon died instantly. I was stunned. What are the odds of that tractor being there at the moment in which Sharon was probably at the height of optimal self-expression, in her bliss station? I'm sure she never saw the tractor.

That evening, after taking the family to the customary local custard stand, I was drawn to the site of Sharon's death. As I slowed down, the kids and Kim were asking me what I was doing. I couldn't speak. They were getting mad at me but I was in another place. Then they realized I was crying and let me be. I pulled over and walked to the optimal self-expression spot, which was marked by a beautiful rainbow someone had drawn on the road. This reminded me of a little picture book my daughter made a number of years ago where she described our family as a rainbow, each of us a different color. It was beautiful. When I was done paying my respects I got back in the van and explained to my family what was going on. I apologized for my behavior. I should have told them why we had come but for some reason I had to feel death for myself first before I could share it as life with the family. That night I couldn't get my mind off of Sharon and so while the rest of the family slept I came up with *The Dancing Light* as my own tribute. Sharon and Kyle are my dancing lights. I want them back. Sometimes I think of them when I feel like giving in to the darkness of the day. I put on my running shoes, go to my sacred place, and offer myself up to athletes like Sharon and Kyle.

The Dancing Light
I had lost my way and was afloat in a sea of darkness
In the distance I could see a light
It seemed to be dancing
Up and down, up and down, up and down
Dancing all around

The dancing light guided my journey
It gave me hope
At times it seemed too far; it's out of reach, I thought

That's when the darkness would come back
But I never lost sight of the dancing light
Up and down, up and down, up and down
Dancing all around

I kept going, not wanting to lose the glimmer of hope
As I got closer to the dancing light,
The darkness faded and I could see for the first time
On the jagged shore was a child
She was all aglow with wonder and movement
Up and down, up and down, up and down
Dancing all around

She reached out her hand
I took it and joined her in the revelry
A brightness came over me that I had never known
I was a dancing light for the first time
Up and down, up and down, up and down
Dancing all around

As we danced
Others, young and old, came to join us
Before long, the shore and all the land was aglow
With dancing lights
Up and down, up and down, up and down
Dancing all around

The sea of darkness gave way to the dancing lights
And never returned
So come join us as we dance
To help us keep the light burning bright
Up and down, up and down, up and down
Dancing all around
Dancing lights every one

Robert Emmons, a psychologist and author of *The Psychology of Grati-tude*, uses a quote from Einstein to highlight the importance of being impacted by others—dead or alive:

A hundred times a day I remind myself that my inner and outer life depends on the labors of other men, living and dead, and that I must exert myself in order to give in the measure as I have received and am still receiving.

I was working my way backwards through an issue of *Sports Illustrated* when near the beginning I caught the word "Died" in "The Blotter" section. I can't explain my seemingly-morbid attraction to the grim reaper but the blurb drew me in as it described how John Boland, 55, an experienced triathlete and computer programmer from Redondo Beach, died by drowning while competing in the Ironman Utah Triathlon at Utah Lake in Provo. The drowning occurred as a result of 40-mph gusts that had created heavy chop. I was thinking that John's death was as bizarre as Sharon's when I realized that Cherie Gruenfeld, whom I had interviewed a few weeks prior, had been competing in the same event. Cherie had been looking forward to Utah as part of her qualifying for the World Championships. I wanted to call to see if she was okay but didn't have the nerve to pick up the phone. I checked her website months later and found that she was out for the remainder of the competitive season as a result of an accident at the Utah Triathlon. I felt terrible. I should have called. Was she one of the swimmers they had to pull out of the water? Was she near John when he died?

Cherie is one of those ageless athletes that inspires while alive. A 7-time age-group winner at the Ironman World Championships, Cherie didn't start running until she was 42 and didn't compete in the Ironman until 1992. She was the first woman over 55 to go under 12 hours in any Ironman race. In case you are wondering, the Ironman is pure physical and mental torture comprised of a 2.4 mile swim, 112 mile bike, and a 26.2 mile marathon.

On a Sunday morning in 1986 Cherie was reading the newspaper's sports section and saw that the LA Marathon was on TV. She turned it on and was mesmerized by the folks running. "I was just envious that they were out there doing something that looked like fun and I was in my house reading the paper and eating sticky buns," Cherie recalls. "I was fascinated by the entire event. I was in awe that these people were testing themselves in that way."

At that moment the athlete within Cherie awoke. She vowed to herself to run in the next LA marathon even though she was not an active runner. In fact, up to that point she poured most of her energy into her job as a computer company executive and did some sporadic skiing and tennis. The very next day she went out and bought her first pair of running shoes and a book on how to run your first marathon.

Her first run was 10 minutes. She progressed rapidly. When asked why or how she says, "I had a goal to run in the LA marathon and that's all there was to it. I didn't intend to become a marathon runner by any means or even to become a runner. I simply was going to run in that LA Marathon. That's it. It took a long time for me to view myself as a runner."

She actually ended up running in a different marathon for her first one and completed it in 3:26, well below her four-hour goal. Her first inclination was to believe that she overachieved.

"I didn't really know what I was doing when I started out," she says. "I didn't train with anyone else. I didn't know anyone that ran. But that first year of running was an awakening for me. I had been in the business world for a number of years and I was always living with someone else's goals that weren't always under my control to achieve. With running, there was nobody or nothing that could come into play that could affect the goal other than me.

Cherie liked the fact that her running put her in charge. At this point she had no idea that she would become an Ironman age-group champion.

"It was kind of exciting to me to discover that I was pretty good at running. And I loved setting a goal and then testing myself in a competitive environment. I just liked being in the game rather than being on the sidelines watching.

Cherie was perfectly content running her marathons, being an athlete. She had read an article about the Ironman in a magazine and thought "this was about the stupidest thing I had ever seen. This is impossible. Just absolutely impossible."

But her husband, Lee, knew her better than that. He kept mentioning the Ironman every now and again but Cherie kept saying that she had no time to train because of work.

Then one of those quirky life events changed everything. Cherie's husband became a best-selling author with his first book *Irreparable Harm*. "Lee came home from signing the book contract," Cherie recalls, "and just laid the thing down in front of me and said, 'Put your money where you mouth is.'"

Cherie took a leave of absence from work and then realized that now she had to learn how to swim and bike to prepare for the Ironman. So the process started all over again. Cherie didn't know she had to qualify. She didn't know anybody who did triathlons. She found out about a coach in San Diego and he agreed to take her on.

"Basically, I just approached it [learning to bike and swim] like I approach everything else in my life," Cherie says. "I just kind of dive in and get to every source I can that tells me how it's supposed to be done and practice. I don't like when I'm not good at something. I don't necessarily enjoy the process of digging in and trying to study it, but there's a goal at the other end, and I can see myself using this stuff and getting better so I can achieve it. That's the enjoyable part."

Cherie's defining moment came when she crossed the finish line of her first Ironman. "I intended to do that race and then go back to the working world in some capacity," she says. "My goal for that first year was fourteen hours. When I crossed the finish line, I looked up at the clock and noticed that it said 26. I crossed the finish line and ran straight into Lee's arms, and said, 'Oh, my God. I finished in 13:26' or 'I finished in under 14!' And he said, 'Are you kidding, you finished in under 13!' I had done it in 12:26. That was so out of the question to me that when I glanced up at the race clock, I just thought it said 13:26. I had just loved the whole day. I loved the process of getting ready for it, the training. I loved the day itself. And so when I ran into his arms, I said to him after we established that I had actually done it in 12:26, 'You know, I don't ever want to go back to work. I love this stuff.' I knew at that point that I would never go back to work."

After that, Cherie started full-blown training and her performances began improving year after year. So what makes Cherie such a great ageless athlete? "I kind of live under the illusion or delusion that it doesn't matter that I'm getting older," she says. "I can always do better. I also love training. If you aren't enjoying the journey, then this is not the sport for you because the workouts would become very onerous as they are time consuming."

Cherie also pays close attention to the specific purpose of every training session—mundanity of excellence. She knows why she's doing it and how it will help her progress toward the big picture of doing well in the Ironman every October.

She prepares mentally as much as, if not more so, than the physical training. The mental and emotional training helps her prepare for the crises that are bound to occur out on the course.

"Racing for 12 hours or so can be very emotional," she says. "Lots of things can go wrong. A great deal of the training is to try and make it so rote and so ready for the race that you can take the emotion out on race day. So instead of panicking when things are going wrong, you can say, 'I've been here before. It's okay. We can get through this.' That's what the training is all about. You can take a lot of those unknowns out of it and you can say, 'Okay, let's think about all the things that could happen to me in the swim.' And you go through it. What's going to happen if some guy smacks me in the head and knocks my goggles off? You want to be so physically and mentally prepared so that race day is just another long day."

Cherie rarely thinks about getting old. She just thinks about getting better. She thinks her late athletic start actually turned into an advantage because physically her body can hold up and mentally she thinks she is a bit wiser than some of her competitors.

She started giving her talent back by coaching some Ironman beginners. She's even taken her passion out to children. Cherie has been working with at-risk school kids through Exceeding Expectations, a foundation she founded to help kids use the sport of triathlon as a way of developing life skills. She helps the kids train for triathlons, even half-marathons, and seeks out sponsors for equipment and donations.

"I really didn't plan on doing this," she says. "I was invited to the school. I just went in and talked to the kids about setting goals and how their lives could go in many different directions but if you set goals and then worked hard and accomplished those goals, that you could do something special with your life. I used the Ironman as a background for this story, and I had a little video. These kids were just wildly enthusiastic about it. One thing just led to another and I love doing it."

That sounds a lot like Cherie's life as an athlete. Once she discovered her passion, she just dove right in to explore it. One thing just led to another and then she was an age-group Ironman champion and then Founder and Director of Exceeding Expectations. And, oh by the way, she has appeared on the box cover of Wheaties.

No one else died in the Utah Triathlon. Why John and not Cherie or some other competitor? Was John's death just bad luck or is there a higher power at work? Was it his time? When and how people die just seems weird to me. As reported by Timothy Carlson in *Inside Triathlon*, the day John died his daughter, her husband, and John's new girlfriend were there watching the event. "Running and triathlon fascinated him," said his daughter. "He loved being outdoors and pushing himself. It made him happy to be able to train and accomplish these goals . . . he had so much energy and so much love for life."

I draw life from Kyle and Sharon and John and Cherie. Their lives are reminders that I'd better get busy living the life of an athlete. As Mel Gibson's William Wallace says in *Braveheart*, "All men die but not all men live."

Think you're too old to be an athlete? Think you're too old to feel alive? Think you're too old to get good? Think again. I'm forever in the debt of these folks for helping me create and sustain the engaged feeling of being alive. Becoming an athlete again has enabled me to sacrifice myself up to them every day. I love them all, dead or alive.

26
ALIGNING GOALS WITH A DREAM

I had about two months as final preparation for running the 1,500 race in Eugene. I still wasn't 100% certain I was going but the idea had grown so big that it seemed to have a life of its own. I can't remember when or how I broached the subject with my wife but I do remember that I used the "will help me write the book" excuse again. I must have timed it perfectly during a moment of weakness or distraction—Kim was either cleaning up Baxter throw up, checking emails, or talking to her mom on the phone. She didn't even seem to mind that I would have to leave for Oregon the day after our 15th wedding anniversary.

I didn't tell her, or anyone, about the PREmonitions I'd been having sporadically throughout the quest. It was Prefontaine who was pulling me out there, and it was so strange that no one would have believed me anyway. Shortly after my online discovery of the Masters Outdoor Championships in the heart of winter, Pre appeared to me again at the Miami track. It was a cold February day and I had cut back on running to give the pain and torture a chance to build me back up. As I was teaching my grad class late in the day, this overwhelming feeling of missing the track came over me. Class was good. I had been able to be myself—goofy, asking questions with no answers, and interacting with the students. Kim was home and she agreed to pick up the kids from childcare so I changed in my office immediately following class and drove to my sacred place. It was about 6:00 p.m., getting dark, and freaking cold with a light snow falling. The gate was locked loose to allow entry—not that it mattered since no one else would be looking to run on the track in this weather. After a mile warm-up, I chose to do eight 200 surges, 200 jogs at a moderate pace and then ended with an up tempo 6:30 mile. It felt darn good. As I warmed down with a walk around the track, a spotlight came on that illuminated the snow falling on the track. As I walked toward the light, this feeling of power and warmth surged through me and then he was there right beside me.

"Hey, Pre, I've been reading up about you."

"Oh, yeah, what do they write about me."

"That no one really understood you. That you were a paradox."

"Well, aren't we all a little misunderstood? Aren't we all a little bit of a paradox."

"Good point. Did you really run a race not to be the fastest but to see who had the most guts, who could punish themselves the most?"

"Yeah, but my belief was that I had the most guts and so I was the only one who could win."

"How did you get guts?"

"Well, people didn't understand that I had to win. I just had to. "

"But why you?"

"To give anything less than your best is to sacrifice the Gift."

"But you also said that 'some people create with words or with music or with a brush and paints. I like to make something beautiful when I run.' How do you combine bleeding, guts, and punishing yourself with creativity and beauty?"

"That's the paradox. That's my Gift. See ya in Eugene."

"But wait, did anyone ever tell you that you look like Jesus Christ. And what really happened the night. . . . "

Pre's ghost was gone. *What is my gift*, I wondered?

I'm not sure running on the track is my gift but it sure does give me the feel I love to have. I was pleased to read that Pre loved the track. "When he [Pre] was on the road, he just ran," teammate and friend Pat Tyson says about him in *Pre* by Tom Jordan, "but he thrived on the track. On the track, he was in his own little world." At least we both have the same sacred place.

Near the end of June, Coach Ceronie actually joined me at the track to guide me through a solo workout—my first-ever private track practice. He loves what he does and I'm getting there. No surprise that I had one of my best workouts as I cruised around the oval doing my 2 x 800, 2 x 400. Coach reminded me to keep the form, keep the head up, and push off on the toes. When I was done, he said, "You are in better condition than you think. Keep your expectations high. You can run sub 4:50 in the 1,500 in Eugene and I think you're close to a 5:15 mile."

I decided it was time to write down a goal: "Get out to Eugene in August and run 4:45 in the 1,500." Based on inspection of the results of previous championship meets, I knew that this time would get me close to qualifying for the finals in the 45-49 age group. I had been avoiding setting a performance goal because, in general, goals are overrated.

Many people who set goals don't know why they are setting them. People think that they will feel a certain way when they reach or achieve the goal. They try to motivate themselves to do a behavior or perform certain acts based on the idea that they will feel real good when the goal is achieved. But goals—even achieving goals—do nothing to enhance our lives unless they are intimately connected to a powerful underlying purpose that emanates from within. Researchers writing in the *Journal of Personality and Social Psychology* call these goals self-concordant—goals that are aligned with one's true self. And they suggest that it is the setting and achieving of these kinds of goals that contribute to long-term motivation and well-being. Most goals, even when achieved, will provide little in the way of fulfillment and meaning unless they're intimately connected to one's self. A lot of internal work has to be done before goals click in enough to motivate. How one feels in the moment of action is a far more powerful source of motivation than are goals. For goals to work, they have to be aligned with a Dream—how you want to feel in the moment of action—and that takes some time.

The best performers choose to do their thing day in and day out not because they believe they'll feel good only when they achieve something, but rather they feel a certain way when they are pursuing a goal. This feeling is then heightened for a short period of time when they actually achieve something. Once they achieve that something, however, the feeling fades quickly if they don't perform again soon. They feel engaged and alive throughout the whole process, not just when they reach their goals. Glenn Close, the actress, says, "The process is the most important thing. If you don't enjoy it, then don't do it." So, no matter what kinds of goals people set, they probably won't achieve them unless they feel certain ways when doing the behaviors relating to the goals. And even if they do achieve the goals, the good feelings are so short-lived that they'd better have a process for getting back to living or they'll feel like hollow men or women.

The key is to pay attention to what makes you feel alive, that feel that helps you optimally express who you are. Living the Dream is the active, dynamic feeling of doing something that is engaging. It is the exercise of freedom in a responsible way. People who live this way feel a good fit between what they are doing and what they value—sometimes called integrity. This fit leads them to feel the way they initially sought to feel or even better. As they progress through the process, they increase their skill level, they get good, which means they need more challenge to stay engaged. They want a continuously dynamic experience, not a static, mundane one. So they prepare better and seek out more difficult challenges or better competition. They set goals.

Many people argue that if they reach their goals then they will feel the way they want to. However, many people who put off their gratification until they achieve something after great personal investment find that the result doesn't feel like they expected it to. It's a major letdown. In addition, for most people, if they don't feel engaged while they're doing something they'll never find out what the achievement will feel like because they lack the energy to achieve it. How you want to feel should decide for you what your goals are.

Throughout this quest, I had spent a lot of time paying attention to how I wanted to feel. The performance goal of 4:45 was a natural result of my experiences.

How you want to feel provides the energy source and goals give direction to that energy. When I was a younger athlete my main problem was that I had tons of energy and passion but didn't get much help in giving that energy direction. As a result my play was typically wild and chaotic. It was fun but many times didn't provide the results that my team or I wanted. The fun about being an older athlete is that I have learned to approach things a little differently now. I can combine self-expression with accomplishment. Expression is the Dream because it allows me to feel the way I want. Accomplishment is important because it gives me more and better chances to pursue that feel. When the two—expression and accomplishment—come together we feel great because our experiences erase the external/internal boundaries that we all struggle with in our everyday existence. When the internal and external become one, we are transcended. We are the hero.

27
TRAINING TRACKS

Due to professional and personal travel, much of July was spent training on tracks in Wisconsin, New Hampshire, and New York. Although all tracks are basically the same, my experiences on them are always a little different.

I was at the National Wellness Conference, and on my day off from presenting I planned to do a 900, 700, 500, 300 interval workout, each at an increasingly faster pace. The previous evening I had made my customary call home. As Kim was telling me about how Baxter threw up again, I heard this scream in the background.

"Something's wrong with Colin," Kim said. "I gotta go."

"Okay, call me back. . . . "

Click.

She called back about 15 minutes later to inform me that Colin had bit his tongue and had been bleeding as if a major artery had ruptured. Kim had the bleeding under control.

"He wants to talk to you," she said. He's probably okay. Just upset.

"Ha, Dathy," my son greeted me.

I had to dig deep to suppress my laughter.

"Hi, son, how are you feeling?"

"Otay, I bit ma tonth."

"I know. Mommy told me. Tongues bleed a lot but it's usually not too serious. You'll probably feel better with a snack and something cold to drink." I was trying my best to be helpful without snickering.

"Dat's what mommy sayth. Loth ya."

"Love you too. I'll see you in a few days."

Something always happens when I go out of town, which is why I don't do that many presentations requiring overnight travel. It's just too hard to leave. There is a lot of preparation (coordinating my travel schedule with Kim's is no fun). Training on the tracks in July was my preparation and it was hard too. But if you're doing it right, preparation is part of the Living the Dream—meaning that preparation (training) can give you all kinds of cool feel. It had better because most athletes spend the greatest chunk of their time in preparation dealing with obstacles of varying sorts. The danger is that you can get stuck in the preparation-obstacle trap—just going back and forth between dealing with obstacles, trying harder, dealing with more obstacles, trying harder. This way of living is a trap because you can lose sight of the Dream over time. I didn't get into this to train. I got into this to feel alive. So I try to get some kind of cool feeling every time I do a track session to remind me that this is about living *my* Dream, not training, not getting better, not working hard.

Here's how my training tracks day unfolded. In the morning, I took a hotel shuttle to the conference center to listen to some keynote speaker talk about real age, which just seemed dumb to me because it had little to do with wellness. I then took the shuttle back to the hotel and changed into my running clothes. Luckily, the conference was being held at the University of Wisconsin, Stevens Point, which had a track accessible to anyone who wanted to self-inflict pain and torture. I packed up my gym bag with bottled water, newspaper, hotel room key, lunch tag, and a towel. I jogged from the hotel to the track, which took about 10 minutes. After more warm-ups and stretching, I busted through the intervals. My pace on each was progressively faster and I was right on my target times. As I warmed-down with a slow jog around the track, my sense of accomplishment was off the charts. I love the feeling of doing something just right, of experiencing something excellent.

Even luckier for me was that lunch was being served in the building directly across from the track. I had timed my intervals so that I would finish in time to grab a bite. I devoured the energy while I read about life in *USA TO-DAY*. The next part of the training tracks day was to jog to the local YMCA, which was offering a $5.00 discounted fee to conference attendees, to lift some weights. About 10 minutes later I arrived at the Y and as I approached the front desk, I realized I had forgotten my money and my wallet was back in my room. My first thought was to say, "Hi, I'm Dr. Jay Kimiecik and I wrote the *YPersonal Fitness Program*, which is used in over 500 YMCAs in North America. Perhaps you've heard of it. I was wondering if I could use your weight room?" I just couldn't bring myself to say such a thing. I went with, "Hi, I'm attending the conference (flashed my badge) and I want to use the weight room but I forgot my money (smiled). "That's alright," the woman at the front desk said. "Just go ahead." I thanked her several times before heading for more pain and torture.

The weight room reminded me of a dungeon and was in one of the old-fashioned fitness centers that hadn't been upgraded. As a consultant, I had been in many Ys over the past five or six years, many of them brand, spanking new. I had forgotten what it was like to be in an old-time weight room. It was hot with little room to maneuver. I got busy doing my routine, being careful not to overdo it since I wasn't familiar with equipment from the dark ages and had just pounded out 2,400 meters. It felt good to be done until I realized I had to jog back to my hotel. Of course, I should have asked someone at the desk how to get to the Holiday Inn but I believed I had a general idea of how to get back. I don't know why I am so delusional as I can get turned around faster than a ballet dancer doing a pirouette. As I began the jog back, I tried to recognize landmarks with little success. There comes a point where even men have to suck it up so I slunk into a florist shop and meekly asked for directions. I don't know how I did it but I had been jogging in the opposite direction of my intended target. It felt good to know where I was going and I enjoyed the slow 20-minute jog back to the hotel. A hot shower and ice for the knees felt even better.

The next day I arrived at the Cincinnati/Northern Kentucky Airport after a long day of travel with a major delay at the Milwaukee Airport. My talk that morning had been well received so this kind of buffered me from the weariness of travel. I was still feeling alive and full of energy as I waited with the other passengers at carousel #4 for our bags to arrive. And waited and waited and waited. We were at #4 because that's where the electronic guide indicated the bags would end up from Flight #1144. After awhile my internal travel antennae were telling me that my wait was beyond normal slowness. So on a hunch I walked across the terminal to check the carousels on the other side. My bags, and probably everyone else's from Flight #1144, were just going round and round on carousel #3. I was ecstatic. I grabbed my two bags and hurried over to tell a few other folks from my flight that their bags were over on carousel #3.

They wouldn't believe me.

"Yes, but it says that the bags are supposed to come out here."

"I know but it's a mistake. Look, I have my bags and I got them on carousel #3."

"Are you sure?"

No, I'm playing a cruel joke on you just for laughs.

"Well, I think I'll wait here a bit longer."

"Okay, good luck."

As I drove by on the shuttle to take me to my car, I could still see the bewildered passengers at carousel #4 . . . waiting . . . waiting . . . waiting. . . .

Becoming an athlete again has helped me be more confident in my instincts. A big part of expressing who you are is to trust yourself and sometimes that will lead to breaking rules or the status quo. One of the migrant workers in *Cider House Rules* told Homer Wells that "sometimes you have to break the rules to make things right." Sometimes other people are wrong, sometimes technology makes mistakes. If you are paying attention to who you are and what you want, you are more likely to trust yourself and be willing to break rules when the occasion calls for it. We get so locked into believing what other people tell us that we can lose our own voice. The little voice just keeps getting smaller and smaller until one day it's gone. The athlete quest has helped me to pay attention, to trust myself, to break rules. My little voice is a lot bigger now.

As I pulled into the driveway, I took a deep breath. There was a lot of work to do to get ready for tomorrow's road trip to New Hampshire. We were going on vacation and I knew that meant a chance to race in New England.

A few days after we arrived at the house we were renting with my parents and two sisters on Little Lake Sunapee in New London, I talked Kim into driving with me up I89 to nearby Lebanon High School for my interval session. The plan was to do 6 x 400 on 4:00 goes at race pace, which I was thinking would be around 75 seconds per lap, which would put me at 3:45 after 3 laps (1200 meters) of the 1500. My plan was to run the last 300 meters in 60 seconds to give me my 4:45.

Kim was my timer and she yelled out "71" after my first 400.

"71, that can't be right," I said. My fastest 400 up to this point had been a 74 on the Miami track.

She showed me the time.

"I just don't think I can be that fast," I said. "Maybe high school tracks are different from college tracks."

For the next one, I started on another line a few yards behind the actual starting line.

"72," Kim shouted.

"72, wow. That was faster than the first one if you take into account where I started."

I started in the same place for the third interval.

"75," Kim said.

"Okay . . . I'm waxed now . . . maybe the first line is right . . . maybe I was just Superman on those first two."

I struggled to 81 and 78 on the next two intervals, which I began at the original starting line, and bagged the last one.

Two nights later, the Kimiecik clan drove up (minus one sister) to the track again for the Twilight Race that was held every Tuesday night throughout the summer. I had stumbled onto the race during one of my late night surfing sessions and after a few email exchanges, the race director confirmed that the event was open to anyone, even New Yorkers via Ohio.

I was there to run the 1600 meters. When I signed in I asked the director, "Is this an official meter track?"

"Sure," he replied. "Why do you ask?"

"Oh, no reason. I was just curious."

"Okay, the kids race first, then the adults."

Carly ran the 50- and 100-meter races. Before Carly's first race, a girl's grandfather told her to shake hands with her competitors. Rachel was 6 and clueless . . . and I have to say so was her grandfather. And then it was time for Carly to run the 1600 (four laps). She started out strong but then got a cramp about midway through. We encouraged her near the end and she finished in 7:58. Carly's got guts. I was impressed. At 10, she's got more runner in her than I'll ever have. I think she's got the Gift.

Then it was my turn. I was up against three high school studs and a guy who appeared to be about my age. My first two laps were 75 and 77, respectively, but I knew I was in trouble. I toiled around the third lap in 84 and totally succumbed to the pain with an 89 on the bell lap (all I could think about was Bill Cosby's comedic description of locking up with rigor mortis during one of his college races). It was my worst performance of the quest and, of course, had been witnessed by my entire family. On the final lap I checked my watch at the 1500 mark and I was at 5:02, 17 seconds slower than my Eugene target. I felt waxed, blasted, blipped, flamed, hosed. I wanted to crawl in a hole and die. I had 2 1/2 weeks to get my act together. *Should I even bother going to Eugene? What would Pre think?*

As we were milling about, everyone was gushing about Carly and she was soaking it up. That took my mind off of my performance until my dad cracked, "You didn't look like a miler out there." Colin followed up with, "You looked slow, dad. Can we go fishing now?" You can always expect brutal honesty from your loved ones. The rest of the week was full of pleasant distractions from my rigor mortis-like performance—saw 4 loons on the lake while kayaking with Carly, played 18 holes of golf with Dad and Colin, caddied for Colin on a par-3 course on the other side of the lake, worked out with Kim at the Hogan Center at Colby Sawyer College, jumped in the cool Sunapee water after runs through New London, and ate lots of ice cream at the local stand.

Thursday night—exactly two weeks to the day that I would need to fly to Oregon—I still hadn't made my flight arrangements. I would need to call before midnight to get the cheapest fare. As the deadline approached, I thought about how much fun I had with my family during the week. Everything seemed so normal. No one would know or care if I decided not to go to the Masters Championships. *Am I doing this to be an athlete or to write a book about it?* Doug had posed this question to me early on. He made me think about the authenticity of what I was doing. *Am I just using running to give me something to write about?* Maybe I was just rethinking all of this because of Tuesday's abysmal performance. But one race does not an athlete make. I probably hadn't recovered from my stupidity with the 400 intervals on Sunday. *Who am I, what do I want?*

The quiet of the night was pierced by the wailing cry of a loon out on the lake. Again, it wailed—oheeeoh, oheeeoh, oheeeoh. Drawn to the mournful song, I walked out into the black and stood at the end of our narrow wooden dock. The Ojibwa tribe thought that the loon's call was an omen of death. Was this a sign that my quest was dead in the water so to speak? I heard the "demoniac laughter" again as Thoreau described the loon's call in *Walden*. Thoreau goes on to say, "This was his looning—perhaps the wildest sound that is ever heard here, making the woods ring far and wide." Maybe it was Pre calling to me. Didn't some people think he was as crazy as a loon? I could just see him howling as he raced, singing his eerie song of death for all his competitors to hear as he massacred them. Pre wailed a few more times and then silence. I stood there in the darkness waiting for more screams but none came. I looked at my watch. Ten minutes to deadline. *Keep the Desire greater than the fear.*

I decided I wasn't ready to die just yet. I made my own call, maybe not as wailing as the loon's but it felt eerie.

A few days later while driving back to Ohio, I thought about a scene in the *Pirates of the Caribbean: The Curse of the Black Pearl* that I had seen with the kids. At some point in the movie, Captain Jack Sparrow and Elizabeth Swann, the token fair maiden, are stranded on an island. They start drinking rum, which leads to some wild ramblings by Captain Jack, who has lost his ship (the Black Pearl) and is desperate to get it back. He tells Elizabeth: "That's what a ship is you know . . . It's not a key in a hole with a deck and sails. That's what a ship needs. But what a ship is . . . what the Black Pearl really is is freedom."

Driving during a long trip can play tricks on your mind but I have to admit that Captain Jack summed up my entire athlete, feeling-alive quest with words spoken in a drunken stupor that I could barely comprehend. When you are totally engaged in something, the feel of being free is at the core of that experience. Let's take this metaphor a little further. What if the ship Captain Jack is talking about is your little voice, your bliss? When I know it and live it, I feel free, I feel autonomous. Without it, I feel lost, trapped, controlled by benevolent oppressors or as A.E Housman writes I am "a stranger and afraid, in a world I never made." I didn't want to be a stranger in a world I never made. I wanted to feel free.

One week before my scheduled flight to Oregon I was on the track with Coach Ceronie for my next to last hard interval set, a 3 x 600 at about race pace with 10-minute recovery in between. Felt awesome. Felt fast. Even I was beginning to believe I could do this. The longer recovery periods between the intervals were part of the performance taper that Coach had suggested. I had never really tapered for anything since I had never really sustained a training regimen long enough for a taper to have much of an effect on my performance. Plus, a taper is usually timed around the biggest meet or event of an athlete's season, and this was my first big event as a burgeoning masters runner. The simple version of the taper is that you progressively cut back on your training—gradually reduce yardage if you are a swimmer, cut-down on mileage if you're a runner. The logic of the taper is also simple. It is designed to keep the mind and body as fresh as possible for maximum performance in the big meet.

Over the next few days, the joy of my taper was interrupted (there's no way to say this delicately) by some rectal irritation. The crack of my butt was really irritated and sore. I've had symptoms like this before and I never know if the irritation is caused by hemorrhoids, anal fissures, or what. Usually, the pain and irritation subside but not this time, which led to a sleepless night. Not taking any chances, the next day I visited my family practitioner who did his customary finger probe to check out the prostate.

"Seems okay to me."

Whew.

"Seems to me that it is some kind of yeast infection," the doc said. "I'll give you prescriptive cream that should clear it up." (I found out after I returned from Oregon that the cause of my symptoms was, in fact, an anal fissure. I won't go into the sordid surgical details).

The next few days were a whirlwind of preparation for the trip to Eugene. I ran 30 minutes easy on Friday. Saturday was a day off so I mowed the lawn and weeded a bit. I also helped Carly and Colin clean their rooms, which at the time seemed to inflict more torture than the third lap of the 1500. On Sunday, I did my final interval work—a 4 x 400 with a one-lap jog in between in 75, 70, 73, 72. It's amazing what a little tapering can do for old legs. Coach told me to do nothing hard until the race on Friday—a few strides and some moderate-paced runs. On Monday, I talked to my friend, Gary, (the same valley guy from my LA race) who now lived in Sisters, Oregon, with his wife and two kids. I was going to stay at their house, which was only a 2-hour drive to Eugene. I also ran 25 minutes on trails. I took the day off on Tuesday. My rectal irritation was still in full force so this had me a little worried. All I could think about was how the weirdest and smallest things impact athletic performance. *Runner fails to achieve PR at Masters Championships due to rectal irritation!* On Wednesday, our wedding anniversary, I spent the morning driving to my favorite running store to pick up my racing singlet. I also gave Kim 15 roses (for putting up with me for 15 years) and bought her some personal training sessions with Luann at the Rec Center. And my greatest gift was that I finally rescheduled my Vasectomy for later in the summer. That evening I packed up and made final preparations—plenty of Vaseline and Aloe for you know what—to head out to Track Town USA. I wished the family was coming with me but it was just too expensive to fly everyone out there. It would just be Pre and me.

28
TRACK TOWN USA

My flight from Cincinnati to Portland was direct and, even better, un-eventful. I don't like flying and enjoy it even less after 9/11. Plus, whenever I fly it reminds me that my son's birthday is on 9/11. I keep trying to put a positive spin on that one and always come up empty. After picking up the rental car, I began the three-hour drive to Sisters, excited and fearful that I would be racing in about 24 hours.

I followed Gary's directions without a hitch (it makes sense to follow some rules) and pulled in to their Sister's driveway in late afternoon. After the customary greetings and house tour, I talked Gary and Hayden into taking me to the local track so I could stretch and do some strides. As we drove through town, Gary gave me the low down on Sisters—once a lumbering town, now known as the Gateway to the Cascades (that is, it's a tourist town). It is beautiful. I love mountains. Kim loves oceans. We live in Ohio. What is wrong with that picture? The high school track/football field is post-cardish, surrounded by pristine pines and snow-capped mountains. "I think they should just move the meet here," I joked to Gary. Hayden, 12, kicked a football around while I stretched. It made me feel good to know that my gut instinct to make the trip to God's Country and Track Town USA had been a good one. My body felt sluggish and, of course, my irritated butt did not like a 4-hour plane ride followed by a 3-hour car journey. I did my 5 or 6 strides of about 150 meters each at a moderate pace, which was the final piece of the taper.

That evening as I neared the point of sleep, I dreamed of running big, only this time the dream felt real. In the morning, the rectal irritation was still there. The prescriptive cream never took effect. All I could do was keep it under control with my assortment of medicinal treatments and ointments. I would have to gut this one out. Hayden and his younger sister, Chloe, were coming along for the ride to Eugene, called "Track Town USA" because of the myriad runners who have flocked there to train over the years—no doubt Pre had a lot to do with making Eugene a sacred place for runners. The drive was very relaxing, full of typical brother-sister bantering. I felt right at home.

A few hours later, as we neared the University of Oregon campus, I was beginning to get a little jittery and impatient. I was hoping that was a sign that my taper was in full force. Gary dropped Hayden and I off at hallowed Hayward Field and he left to take Chloe to a friend's house. We found the registration building and after checking in looked at the list of 29 runners— the most of any age group—who had preregistered in my age group. I knew I was in trouble—they only take 12 runners for the finals and I would be near the bottom third of the performance ladder.

Around noon I checked in at the clerks table, which is the official registration spot for each race.

"You make 12," the volunteer in charge said.

"What does that mean?"

"Well, if we get 16 we race the prelims. If not, no prelims and you're off until Sunday afternoon. Check back in an hour and we can give you an update."

That would be a bummer if I had to wait till Sunday to race. I hadn't planned on that.

"Don't worry," the official said, "We only need four more and we've got plenty of time."

Gary had returned and we sat in the stands to watch the 100-meter prelims, which seemed to go on and on and on. You can tell the studs from the nobodies like me. They carry themselves different, with a swagger. I tried to imagine what it would have been like to watch Pre run around this very track. He once had 1,000 fans show up just to watch him run a tune up mile in preparation for a race in Europe. According to the story, he coughed up blood afterwards due to smoke from farmers burning ground cover. I was hoping that he was around somewhere. I needed to feel his presence.

And then it was time for my race.

Pre, where are you?

I toed the starting line of my 1,500-meter qualifying heat with nine other 45-49 year old feel seekers at the USA Masters Outdoor Track and Field Championships. My head was filled with nagging thoughts and questions: *Am I a real runner? Who are these guys? They look damn serious and damn good. Where are you, Pre?*

The gun went off. I immediately fell near the back of the pack, as I knew I would. *Relax. No big deal.* I cruised the first lap in 76, just a second over my goal pace. I was in last place but that didn't bother me. *This seems pretty easy. I'm used to racing against myself anyway.*

Keep the pace. Stay strong. Stay smooth. This is starting to hurt. The pain means nothing. It's a sign you're pushing. That's what you want. I was still in last place but not far behind the guy just in front of me. *Keep him close. Man, my throat is dry.* Two laps down and the electronic timer showed 2:32. *Okay, another 76. Good pace. Stay tall. Here we go. The pain is coming. . . .*

This hurts so much, I want to quit. Why would anyone voluntarily succumb to this pain and torture? At least I'm not going to be lapped. Stay tall, stay strong, hold on. Stay with this guy. Maybe you can pass him on the last lap. My lungs are going to burst. Embrace the pain, Jay, embrace the pain.

At the end of lap three I was at 3:48. *Another 76. Great job. Three hundred meters to go and the pain is over. Hold on. I'm losing it. Help me, Pre. Help me, God. Someone help me.*

A heaviness came over me on the backstretch unlike any I have ever known. I felt as if death was near. And then I was on the home stretch—the final 100 meters—and I felt lighter as if someone was carrying me along. But it was too late. I had lost too much time in the previous 200 meters. I imagined myself flying. I tried to catch the guy in front of me. Too late.

4:52—a personal best but too slow to qualify for the finals.

After a light lunch at a restaurant just around the corner from Hayward Field, I asked Gary to drive me to Alton Baker Park so I could take a slow, solitary jog on Pre's Trail. As we drove by Hayward Field on our way out, Hayden, sitting in the back, said, "Hey, Jay, I was kind of surprised that there weren't more scientists here today studying the athletes."

I had shared my story with Hayden earlier about my interest in studying and learning more about masters athletes. So I thought he was referring to that discussion.

"Why is that, Hayden? I replied, quite impressed with his interest.

"Because it's quite rare to see fossils in action."

I laughed and laughed and laughed. I just couldn't stop laughing. It was the funniest joke I had heard in a long time, the brainchild of a 12-year old. I laughed so hard that I missed saying bye to Hayward Field.

We pulled into the parking lot of the Park, which was situated along the banks of the Willamette River, and walked across the bridge to read about how Pre's Trail came to be. Pre had discovered trail running when training in Europe and when he returned to the states had tried unsuccessfully to lobby the city of Eugene to construct a wood chip running trail. The trail was approved one day after he died.

"Do you want us to come with you," Gary asked.

"Na, this is something I need to do myself," I said.

"Okay, we're going to take a quick walk over to the football stadium."

"I shouldn't be more than 15 or 20 minutes," I said.

Alone again, I started down the trail, and there he was.

"Well, Pre, I'm glad you decided to join me. Where were you when I needed you?" I asked.

"I was watching," Pre said. "You got guts kid."

"Yeah, but I didn't qualify."

"Don't look for sympathy from me, man. When I was running someone like you would have been a bug on my windshield. Plus, you know you didn't do this race to qualify."

"It would have been nice."

"But how do you really feel right now, at this moment?"

"I feel alive," I said.

"Right. That's how I felt when I ran. I had lots of disappointments in my career. There were times when I questioned what I was doing. Over the years, I'd given myself a thousand reasons to keep running, but it always came back to where it started. It came down to self-satisfaction and a sense of achievement."

"Dreams and goals," I said.

"Right. I loved watching you suffer on that backstretch. It reminded me of why I loved running so much. It reminded me of my dream of pure guts at the end. You didn't handle it too well but you did pull it together at the end."

"Yeah, I felt lighter on the home stretch."

"Like you had somebody helping you?"

"Yeah . . . hey, was that you."

"I don't know what you're talking about."

"Sonofagun, Pre. That was you."

"Yeah, well don't tell anybody. I had some help. Plus, I don't want people thinking I was a nice guy. It'll ruin my image. Well, I gotta get going. Other bliss seekers are calling."

"You know about bliss?"

"I lived it till the day I died."

"Joseph Campbell, another friendly ghost, says that when you live your bliss, your passion, you are helped by invisible hands, like today on the home stretch. You helped me and I didn't even realize it."

"Yeah, well I don't know about any of that stuff. I just loved what I did and tried to help others when I could. I wasn't perfect. I must go. You don't need ghosts anymore."

"Thanks, Pre." I started crying. "What should I do now?"

But he was gone.

On the flight back home, I had about 4 hours to reflect on what I was bringing back with me. Athletes like Pre go for the pure engagement, the feeling of being totally alive. I feel that's what I'm bringing back. You don't have to be an outstanding runner to feel rapture—I finished 18 out of 20 in the 1,500 prelims at the US Masters Outdoor Track and Field Championships. Heroes go for something and on the way they face many trials and tribulations to determine if they are worthy. I had to slay lots of dragons—achievement, fear, and responsibility, to name a few. And I did that by making my little voice BIG! But most of all, I had to take the journey to kill the rational, the textbook, the averages. That's what I felt on the backstretch of the Hayward Field track. My rapture had gotten so big that at that moment the ordinary in me died. And then the hidden hands of Pre brought me back to life on the home stretch. Campbell says,

> We are in childhood in a condition of dependency under someone's protection and supervision for some fourteen to twenty one years—and if you're going on for your Ph.D., this may continue to perhaps thirty-five. You are in no way a self-responsible, free agent, but an obedient dependent, expecting and receiving punishment and rewards. To evolve out of this position of psychological immaturity to the courage of self-responsibility and assurance requires a death and a resurrection. That's the basic motif of the universal hero's journey—leaving one condition and finding the source of life to bring you forth into a richer or mature condition.

A death *and* a resurrection. And that's why Pre had been calling me out to Eugene—to help kill off the part of me that I was hanging on to but didn't need anymore. And then my bliss took over, bringing me back to life—leaving one condition and finding the source of life for a richer condition. I am forever changed, forever transformed.

Pre's ghost was right. I don't need ghosts anymore. I am now one of them.

I am now alive.

ACKNOWLEDGEMENTS

Runner as Hero would never have seen the light of day without some special people who graciously gave their time to guide my inner quest of feeling alive as a masters athlete of sorts. Many experts agreed to be interviewed either by phone or in person. Some key experts on the science side of things were Dr. David Costill, Dr. Steve Devor, and Dr. Peter Weyand. Special thanks to Dr. Devor at Ohio State University for conducting my VO_2 max tests and taking the time to help me understand the relationship between aging, training, and muscle physiology. I also interviewed many masters athletes and their stories inspired me in ways they'll never know. I want to especially thank Marie-Louise Michelsohn and Cherie Gruenfeld for sharing their stories with me.

Many Miami University students helped me research the scientific literature on aging, training, and performing but Kylee Studer was most helpful as she transcribed the masters athlete interviews and my journals as well as organized all of my "stuff." Nicole Taylor and Chris Manhart were excellent student trainers. And thanks to Joyce Englander who helped write up the Jeff Rouse story.

Thanks to Dr. Rich Ceronie, former Head Women's Track & Field Coach at Miami University, and all of his middle-distance runners who welcomed me as part of the team. Dr. Ceronie's assistance in guiding my training as well as helping me run faster than I ever thought possible is greatly appreciated. Thanks also to Dan Dalrymple for taking the time to test my strength—and not laugh about my initial results.

Pete Zulia and Mark Cristell, my physical therapists, deserve special mention for keeping me running when I probably had no business doing so. And Lara Freidline did a great job guiding my aqua therapy. Stacy Osborne, my podiatrist and an avid runner, helped me get on track with great orthotics and great music.

I want to thank Gary Stein, my long-time friend, and his family for hosting me during my sojourn to compete and have my final chat with Pre's ghost in Oregon. On the family front, my wife, Kim, and two children, Carly and Colin, were very patient and supportive throughout my quest, especially when I told them I was running in yet another weekend race. I hope they realize they are heroes too.

Lastly, I want to thank Doug Newburg for introducing me to the idea and experience of feel, and for being a good friend.

REFERENCES

Bortz, W. IV & Bortz, W. II. 1996. How fast do we age? Exercise performance over time as a biomarker. *Journal of Gerontology, 51A*, M223-M225.

Campbell, J. 1988. *The power of myth*. New York: Doubleday.

Carron, A., & Leith, L. 1986. Psychology of the masters athlete: Motivational considerations. In Brock, R., & Sutton, J, editors, *Sports medicine for the mature athlete*, Indianapolis, IN: Benchmark Press.

Chambliss, D. 1989. The mundanity of excellence: An ethnographic report on stratification and Olympic swimmers. *Sociological Theory, 7*, 70-86.

Chouinard, Y. 2000. Climber's bill of rights. In *Voices from the summit*. Washington, D.C.: Adventure Press, 95-99.

Costill, D., & Trappe, S. 2002. *Running: The athlete within*. Traverse City, MI: Cooper Publishing Group.

Dufek, J. (2002, July/August). Exercise variability: A prescription for overuse injury prevention. *ACSM's Health and Fitness Journal*, 6, 18-23.

Emmons, R., & McCullough, M. 2004. *The psychology of gratitude*. Oxford University Press.

Ericsson, K. 2003. Development of elite performance and deliberate practice. In Starkes, J., & Ericsson, K., editors, *Expert performance in sports*, Champaign, IL: Human Kinetics, 49-83.

Fillit, H., et al. 2002. Achieving and maintaining cognitive vitality with aging. *Mayo Clinic Proceedings, 77*, 681-696.

Gladwell, M. (1999, August). The physical genius. *The New Yorker*, 57-65.

Hall, S. 2002. *Drawn to the rhythm: A passionate life reclaimed*. New York: W. W. Norton & Company.

Harper, B. 1979. Man alone. In Gerber, E., & Morgan, W., editors, *Sport and the body*. Philadelphia, PA: Lea & Febiger, 125-127.

Jerome, J. 1984. *Staying with it: On becoming an athlete*. New York: Viking Press.

Jones, L. 2002. Mundane excellence. *Christian Century*. Retrieved from http://www.findarticles.com. [Accessed 3 December 2003].

Jordan, T. 1997. *Pre*. Rodale.

Leonard, G. 1974. *The ultimate athlete*. New York: Viking.

Leonard, G. 1991. *Mastery: The keys to long-term success and fulfillment*. New York: Dutton.

Lieber, J. 2003, March 11. Retirement offers 'freedom to follow dream.' *USA TODAY*.

Maharam, L., et al. 1999. Masters athletes: Factors affecting performance. *Sports Medicine, 28*, 273-285.

Markey, K. 2001, March 16-18. At 50+ they (still) got game. *USA Weekend*.

Maron, B., et al. 2001. Recommendations for preparticipation screening and the assessment of cardiovascular disease in masters athletes. *Circulation, 103*. http://www.circ.ahajournals.org [Accessed 26 November 2001].

McCammon, R. 1992. *Boy's life*. New York: Pocket.

Messner, R. 2000. A passion for limits. In *Voices from the summit*. Washington, D.C.: Adventure Press, 221-225.

Metheny, E. 1979. The symbolic power of sport. In Gerber, E., & Morgan, W., editors, *Sport and the body*. Philadelphia, PA: Lea & Febiger, 231-236.

Newburg, D., Kimiecik, J., Durand-Bush, N, & Doell, K. 2002. The role of resonance in performance excellence and life engagement. *Journal of Applied Sport Psychology, 14*, 249-267.

Paavolainen, L., et al. 1999. Explosive-strength training improves 5-k running time by improving running economy and muscle power. *Journal of Applied Physiology, 86*, 1527-1533.

Palmer, P. 1999. *Let your life speak: Listening for the voice of vocation*. San Francisco, CA: Jossey-Bass.

Pelletier, K. 1994. *Sound mind, sound body*. New York: Simon & Schuster.

Pirsig, R. 1974. *Zen and the art of motorcycle maintenance*. New York: William Morrow and Company.

Pollock, M., et al. 1997. Twenty-year follow-up of aerobic power and body composition of older track athletes. *Journal of Applied Physiology, 82*, 1508-1516.

Rowe, J., & Kahn, R. 1998. *Successful aging*. New York: Dell Publishing.

Ryan, R., & Deci, E. 2001. On happiness and human potentials: A review of research on hedonic and eudaimonic well-being. *Annual Review of Psychology 52*, 141-166.

Schul, B. 2000. *Psychology of competition* [online]. Available from: http://www.bob-schul.com [Accessed 17 October 2002].

Seven, R. *Underwater running*. Available from: http://www.azstarnet.com. [Accessed 7 April 2004].

Sheldon, K., Ryan, R., Deci, E., & Kasser, T. 2004. The independent effects of goal contents and motives on well-being: It's both what you pursue and why you pursue it. *Personality and Social Psychology Bulletin, 30*, 475-486.

Sterken, E. 2003. From the cradle to the grave: how fast can we run? *Journal of Sports Sciences, 21*, 479-491.

Weston, A., et al. 1999. African runners exhibit greater fatigue resistance, lower lactate accumulation, and higher oxidative enzyme activity. *Journal of Applied Physiology, 86*, 915-923.

ABOUT THE AUTHORS

JAY KIMIECIK, PHD, is a professor at Miami University (Oxford, Ohio) and founder of the Well-Being Way. His early work pioneered the integration of behavior change theory with optimal experiences to enhance understanding of physical activity across the lifespan. He also developed and tested the Family Influence Model, which extended the study of children's physical activity from descriptive to more conceptual- and theory-based. Because of this groundbreaking work, Jay was awarded the prestigious *Research Writing Award* by the American Alliance for Health, Physical Education, Recreation and Dance. He is the author of *The Intrinsic Exerciser: Discovering the Joy of Exercise* and wrote the *YPersonal Fitness Program (YPFP)* for the YMCA of the USA, a behavior change program for beginning exercisers that utilizes an innovative personal coach model. The YPFP has been used in over 500 YMCAs in North America. His most recent work, funded by the WellPoint Foundation, explores the connection between purposeful and healthy living for high school and college students and teachers. Jay received his BS from SUNY Cortland, an MS from Purdue University, and his PhD in exercise and sport psychology from the University of Illinois at Champaign-Urbana. He lives in Oxford, Ohio, with his sports-minded family.

DOUG NEWBURG, PHD, is the co-founder of Powered by Feel. He has interviewed and worked with hundreds of world-class performers in fields as diverse as sports, business, aeronautics, the military, and education. Doug was on the general faculty at the University of Virginia Medical School for 15 years where he was named to the Academy of Distinguished Medical Educators, and he worked for several years at the University of Florida Medical School in the thoracic surgery division. He is the author of *The Most Important Lesson No One Every Taught Me, A Pearl's Promise,* and *Powered By Feel.* He was featured in John Eckberg's book, *The Success Effect: Uncommon Conversations with America's Business Trailblazers,* and has appeared on *Good Morning America.* His work has been cited in publications including *Outside, Self, Reader's Digest, Olympic Coach,* and *GQ.* He shares his time between Colorado and Florida, loves movies, reading, and almost any sport. Doug played basketball at the University of Virginia and continues to be active by bicycling and rollerblading a hundred miles a week.